Shackles of Iron

Slavery Beyond the Atlantic

D1216537

Series Editor: Alfred J. Andrea
Emeritus Professor of History
University of Vermont

Shackles of Iron

Slavery Beyond the Atlantic

Stewart Gordon

Hackett Publishing Company, Inc.
Indianapolis/Cambridge

For further information, please address
    Hackett Publishing Company, Inc.
    P.O. Box 44937
    Indianapolis, Indiana 46244-0937

    www.hackettpublishing.com

Cover design by Rick Todhunter
Interior design by Elizabeth L. Wilson
Composition by Aptara, Inc.

Library of Congress Cataloging-in-Publication Data
Names: Stewart, Gordon T. (Gordon Thomas), 1945– author.
Title: Shackles of iron : slavery beyond the Atlantic / Stewart Gordon.
Description: Indianapolis : Hackett Publishing Company, Inc., [2016] |
    Series: Critical themes in world history | Includes bibliographical
    references and index.
Identifiers: LCCN 2015035373| ISBN 9781624664748 (pbk.) |
    ISBN 9781624664755 (cloth)
Subjects: LCSH: Slavery—History.
Classification: LCC HT861 .S74 2016 | DDC 306.3/6209—dc23
LC record available at http://lccn.loc.gov/2015035373

CONTENTS

SERIES EDITOR'S FOREWORD

Sunk into the ground outside the Anglican cathedral of Christ Church in Zanzibar City, Tanzania, is a concrete memorial by the Swedish sculptor Clara Sörnäs. The five doleful, utterly defeated individuals depicted in the sculpture represent the vast numbers of enslaved human beings who passed through the archipelago of Zanzibar over the course of many centuries. The photo that serves as the cover for this book shows one of those five, a woman wearing a neck chain. That is an actual nineteenth-century slave chain worn by slaves who traveled to and through this island on their dehumanizing journey from homes in Africa's interior.

In 1873, British authorities, employing diplomacy and the power of the Royal Navy, persuaded the sultan of Zanzibar to declare an end to the centuries-old, seaborne slave trade that emanated from the two major islands of his sultanate, Unguja (popularly known as Zanzibar, and the island on which Zanzibar City is located) and Pemba. In celebration of that abolitionist victory, Bishop Edward Steere began construction, in that same year, of a new cathedral church on the site of the former slave market. The high altar of the cathedral was placed immediately behind where the whipping tree had been located. Following an age-old practice, male slaves were chained to the tree and whipped in the presence of potential buyers in order to demonstrate their strength and endurance.

Prior to being auctioned off, slaves were held in fetid underground holding cells with essentially no light, little or no fresh air, and precious little space for movement. Today all that remains of that slave market are two holding cells. Here slaves were segregated by sex and age—women and children in a larger cell, men in a smaller chamber.

The sultan's decree ending Zanzibar's seaborne slave trade did not end slavery in his domain. Zanzibar's clove, sugar, and indigo plantations continued to absorb large numbers of slaves. Reputedly, Tippu Tip (1837–1905), a wealthy ivory and slave trader who resided in Zanzibar City, had ten thousand slaves on his plantations. Indeed, the ivory and slave trades had been intimately connected for centuries inasmuch as newly enslaved persons carried ivory from the interior as they were herded to the slave markets of the Swahili Coast of East Africa.

Seaborne slave trading from Zanzibar also continued to flourish by going underground—metaphorically and literally. Underground slave

The basement of Christ Church, Zanzibar City, Tanzania. This cell, reserved for women and children, held about eighty slaves. The channel in the middle of the room was for human waste. The two side windows are modern constructions. When used as a slave pen, the cell had only a single small window. Photo courtesy of A. J. Andrea.

pens were constructed in remote, forested areas from which slaves would be secretly shipped out at night to far-away locations.

Supposedly slavery in Zanzibar and in many other locations along the Swahili Coast effectively ended in the wake of World War I. But did it ever end? Today this region of the East African coast is a major entrepôt for the exportation of child slaves.

As Stewart Gordon brilliantly demonstrates in this little book, slavery is a phenomenon at least as old as our earliest civilizations. Moreover, it was, until fairly recent days, universally accepted as a normal human state, and by virtue of having taken root in almost every human culture, it has taken on a wide variety of forms and faces. In other words, the trans-Atlantic slave trade and slavery in the Americas, especially in the Antebellum South, should not be viewed as representing the totality of human bondage, human trade, and human exploitation. When it comes to slavery as viewed across the vast expanses of time and space, one size does not fit all, and one form of slavery cannot stand as a model of all slavery.

A remote underground slave pen on Unguja (Zanzibar Island). Photo courtesy of A. J. Andrea.

A book of this size cannot claim to offer a comprehensive history of slavery around the world from antiquity to the present. It can and does, however, present four case studies that suggest by their diversity the complex realities of slavery.

Following an introduction that sketches in broad strokes slavery as viewed both historically and anthropologically, Gordon introduces us to slavery in ancient Athens, a *polis* that evolved one of the world's purest forms of participatory democracy, but that democratic freedom was borne on the backs of slaves, both Hellenes and non-Hellenes alike.

Every American schoolchild has heard and read about the traffic in slaves that emanated out of West Africa and flooded the Americas with human chattel. Few Americans, however, even well-educated ones, know of the East African trade in slaves, which thrived for many more centuries than that of the West African coastal kingdoms and for which Zanzibar served as a primary locus. As Gordon admits, unlike the voluminous shipping and commercial records available for scholars studying the trans-Atlantic slave trade, reliable data do not exist that allow historians to estimate how many humans were forcibly transported to and out of the coastal cities of East Africa, but there is no doubt that they numbered in the millions.

Slavery in the North African states known as Barbary was likewise quite different from that of the Americas. The ballad "High Barbaree," which celebrates the victory of a British or American (there are two versions) man-o'-war over a Barbary pirate ship, was more wishful thinking than reality. As Gordon notes, the state-sponsored capture and enslavement by Barbary pirates of largely Christian European seafarers along the Mediterranean and Atlantic coasts of the Maghrib (western North Africa) in the period from roughly 1500 to the late eighteenth century was a huge and highly profitable business that resulted in a form of slavery that encouraged the ransom of many of these white-skinned captives—at least those fortunate enough to escape a short-lived career as a galley slave. And how many enslaved Europeans (and later Americans) are we talking about? A reasonable estimate is anywhere from a million to a million and a half in the period from about 1530 to the 1780s.

Some U.S. history textbooks briefly note the two Barbary wars, in which the fledgling U.S. Navy engaged these temporarily rejuvenated pirate states in 1801–1805 and 1815, and every U.S. Marine recruit has heard the story of the heroic exploits of Lieutenant Presley O'Bannon and seven other marines who traveled "to the shores of Tripoli." Nevertheless, the fuller story of Barbary slavery is largely unknown today in America and Europe. Chapter 3 of this book, "Slavery along the Barbary Coast," remedies that omission in our general storehouse of historical knowledge.

Many readers of this book will probably also be unaware of the widespread existence of slavery around the world (including the United States) in the twenty-first century. As Chapter 4 informs us, given the size of the human population and the varied, often ingenious ways in which people are held in involuntary servitude today, there are probably more slaves across the globe today than ever before in the course of world history—despite a general consensus that slavery is unnatural and immoral, and notwithstanding the best attempts of governments and supragovernmental organizations, such as the United Nations, to eradicate this multiheaded evil.

Lest he leave the reader in despair, Gordon ends his epilogue, "Reflections and Conclusions," with some practical advice of how we, individual citizens, can engage in the effort to eradicate slavery.

Indeed, reflections and at least provisional conclusions are asked of the reader in every chapter. Consonant with all books in the Critical Themes in World History series, each of this book's four case studies provides four primary sources, each preceded by a list of "Questions for Consideration" that require the reader to probe more deeply into the form of historic slavery under consideration. Through such analysis, the reader becomes an active inquirer into the complex and highly variegated issue of slavery.

In conclusion, this is an important book that should be read and pondered over by every student of world history.

Alfred J. Andrea
Series Editor

ACKNOWLEDGMENTS

A book of this scope depends on the expertise of colleagues. I wish to acknowledge colleagues who discussed aspects of or formally critiqued chapters: Richard Eaton, Collin Ganio, Juan Cole, Patrick Manning, Stephen Morillo, and Lee Schlessinger. I appreciate the chance to present portions of the book in public lectures at the University of Pittsburgh and the Center for South Asian Studies at the University of Michigan. I wish to thank Karl Longstreth and Tim Utter of the University of Michigan Map Collection, the curators and staffs of the University of Michigan Rare Book Room, the Cleveland Public Library, the Library of Congress Prints and Photographs Department, the Newberry Library, and the American Geographical Society Collection at the University of Wisconsin-Madison. The close reading by Al Andrea, series editor, assisted the intellectual development of the book. The financial support of the Helen and John S. Best Fellowship and the Earhart Foundation made the research possible.

PREFACE

School and community college teachers in my workshops on worldwide slavery are asked to close their eyes and shout out the first image that comes into their mind in response to a string of words. *Slave* evokes a slave ship, a plantation, and blacks hoeing rows of cotton. *Master* evokes a white man on horseback, a whip, and a mansion. *Freedom* evokes Harriet Tubman, "Amazing Grace," the Underground Railway, and the Haitian Rebellion. These images are so thoroughly and widely shared that I can predict them even before the exercise begins.

For Americans, slavery is Atlantic slavery, especially as practiced in the Antebellum South. Our images come from Hollywood movies, TV series, novels, and school textbooks. In addition, thousands of books and articles have analyzed the political, economic, regional, sociological, and psychological aspects of the trans-Atlantic slave trade and slavery in the Americas. If there is anything that teachers and students already know about slavery in the world, it is Atlantic slavery. I have, therefore, consciously chosen not to discuss Atlantic slavery in this book. Instead, it focuses on slavery in the rest of the world, a subject largely unnoticed and not taught in either schools or colleges.

This larger perspective turns many accepted truths about slavery into questions. How common, in fact, was plantation slavery? How often was slavery connected to race? Were slaves always cut off from their families, or was this unusual? Were slaves routinely transported over long distances? How often were slaves freed, and what were the processes of gaining freedom?

Many of the answers to these questions surprise college and high school teachers in my workshops, challenging much of what they thought they knew about slavery. The ubiquitous practice of slavery across the world and through time (and into our present day) is in some sense even more tragic than Atlantic slavery. The worldwide declarations of the immorality of slavery, however, are perhaps signals of more hope than the continuing racism in America suggests. Overall, we need to understand slavery in history and the world both as a context for Atlantic slavery and to arm us in the struggle against the ugly remnants of slavery in our modern world.

Stewart Gordon

INTRODUCTION

The Origins and Nature of Slavery

Our images of slavery come from the Americas and include field labor on cotton and sugar plantations, white masters and black slaves, a densely crowded slave ship, and heroes leading slaves to freedom. These images rest on thousands of academic studies of Atlantic slavery on such topics as the logistics and economics of the trade, cultural transfer and creolization, resistance and abolition movements, the complex gender issues of slavery, and visual and literary representations of slaves. The more direct source for common images of slavery has been such popular Hollywood movies as *Gone with the Wind* and *Amistad*. The unfortunate result of this intense focus on Atlantic slavery is to emphasize its unique, special, and "peculiar" character.

Slavery was, however, not a singular phenomenon of European colonialism. It has been characteristic of every continent and every historic time period in a wide variety of societies, including herding, agricultural, and industrial cultures. Slavery began before the writing of human records and remains with us today.

The Origins of Slavery

During the many millennia when humans were solely hunters and gatherers, it is unlikely that there were slaves because the population was quite sparse. Opportunities for capturing prisoners were limited, and there was little advantage to enslaving a person who did not know the microclimate well enough to produce a surplus of gathered food.

Scholars have speculated that slavery appeared at the same time as the first domestication of plants and animals, termed the Global Neolithic Revolution, which took place in sub-Saharan Africa, China, Southeast Asia, and the Americas about ten thousand years ago, and apparently earlier in Southwest Asia (the Middle East). Humans attempted to domesticate a host of animals during this period of early agriculture but succeeded with only a few: sheep, cattle, chickens, goats, pigs, horses, and geese. Earlier, they had domesticated dogs. These successful domesticates

Slaves destined for the plantations of the Americas. A depiction of the West African slave trade in the anti-slavery book by William Blake, *The History of Slavery and the Slave Trade, Ancient and Modern* (1860). (CC-BY-SA 3.0 license.)

were all social animals, grazing or hunting in groups, and each species had a dominance hierarchy. Humans discovered that they could insert themselves at the top of the dominance hierarchy and have these animals mostly obey. Perhaps slaves were considered another sort of animal, also social and hierarchical, and thus were able to be domesticated and dominated with threatened and actual violence.[1]

The Neolithic Revolution resulted in field crops and herds producing the majority of human food. Labor, especially field and domestic labor, was a scarce, expensive resource. The debate over the connection between the worldwide development of agriculture and the emergence of societal subordination is now more than a century old but still has strong advocates on both sides. Agriculture had its "benefits" and its "costs." Those who emphasize the benefits correctly correlate the development of agriculture with the emergence of urban centers, states, art, philosophy, literature, and a courtly culture. Those who emphasize the costs see crushing taxation on the peasants, the subordination of women, and the likelihood of periodic famines as the inevitable downside of agriculture. A middle ground might accept both sides of the argument. Controlling labor was virtually the only way to create personal, family, and other group wealth in these early societies. The elites, therefore, evolved a variety of methods to keep cultivators on

1. Karl Jacoby, "Slaves by Nature? Domestic Animals and Human Slaves," *Slavery and Abolition* 15 (1994): 89–97.

the land for the yearly round of planting and harvesting. Some exploitative strategies were short run and even destructive, but many societies evolved strategies of subordination that were sustainable in the long run.

Slavery was one solution to this problem of controlling scarce and valuable labor. Across the world slaves have performed much of both the ordinary labor in agriculture and herding and the hard, dangerous labor in mines, galleys, large-scale plantations, construction, and road building. Much of the drudgework in households—cleaning, food preparation, laundry, and carrying water—has been slave labor. Slaves have also been the soldiers in many armies, teachers in the households of elites, concubines in upper-class households, overseers of other slaves, and even civil officials endowed with a high degree of authority.

Slaves were not simply domesticated animals, much as some philosophers, slave merchants, and owners might try to consider and treat them as such. The very humanity of slaves involved them with the family and society that held them in a complex web of power, impotence, lust, affection, loyalty, fear, and hope. The earliest descriptions of slavery were embedded in the law codes of early agricultural states, such as the *Code of Hammurabi* (ca. 1750 BCE) from Mesopotamia. Consider this group of laws about runaway slaves:

> If a man seize a male or female slave, a fugitive, in the field and bring that (slave) back to his owner, the owner of the slave shall pay him two shekels of silver.
>
> If that slave will not name the owner, he shall bring him to the palace and they shall inquire into his antecedents and they shall return him to his owner.
>
> If he detain that slave in his house and later the slave be found in his possession, that man shall be put to death.
>
> If the slave escapes from the hand of the captor, that man shall so declare, in the name of god, to the owner of the slave and shall go free.[2]

Laws such as these suggest that slaves resisted their plight and fled. Even when caught they sometimes refused to give the name of their

2. Robert Francis Harper, *The Code of Hammurabi, King of Babylon, about 2250 B.C.* (Chicago: University of Chicago Press, 1904), 17.

master. They also ran away, if they could, from the person who caught them. The draconian punishment of death for harboring a runaway slave suggests that sometimes families offered refuge in return for the slave's labor.

Again, consider the *Code of Hammurabi* and its assumption of sexual relations between master and female slave.

> If a man's wife bear him children and his maid-servant bear him children and the father during his lifetime say to the children which the maid-servant bore him: "My children" and reckon them with the children of his wife, after the father dies, then the children of the wife and the children of the maid servant shall divide the goods of the father's house equally. The child of the wife shall have the right of choice at the division.
>
> But if the father during his lifetime has not said to the children which the maid servant bore him: "My children," after the father dies, the children of the maid servant shall not share in the goods of the father's house with the children of the wife. The maidservant and her children shall be given their freedom. The children of the wife may not lay claim to the children of the maidservant for service.[3]

Another messy problem at the center of slavery was how to prevent escaped slaves from merging invisibly into the general population and even guaranteeing that a freed ex-slave could be easily recognized. Many societies scarred the face or cut the ears of a slave so that, even if escaped or freed, he or she could always be identified. The *Code of Hammurabi*, taking a more compassionate approach, anticipated that many slaves would enter society and function as free individuals, and therefore forbade facial scarring of a slave who stayed with a single family until freed.

Laws in the Torah (the first five books of the Hebrew Bible), which were compiled quite a bit later than the *Code of Hammurabi*, suggest that different routes to slavery offered different possibilities for freedom. The Book of Deuteronomy, which dates probably from the seventh century BCE but undoubtedly reflects the laws and practices of earlier Israelite

---

3. Ibid., 61.

history, makes clear that female war captives from distant cities could expect permanent slavery, as could their children.

> When the LORD your God delivers it into your hand, put to the sword all the men in it. As for the women, the children, the livestock and everything else in the city, you may take these as plunder for yourselves. And you may use the plunder the LORD your God gives you from your enemies. This is how you are to treat all the cities that are at a distance from you and do not belong to the nations nearby.[4]

In contrast, laws in the somewhat later Book of Leviticus (probably the fifth century BCE) pronounce that local impoverished Hebrews who sold themselves into slavery could expect relatively benign treatment and freedom for themselves and their children after anywhere from one to forty-eight years, depending on when they entered into bondage in relation to the Year of Jubilee, which came every forty-nine years, being the sum of seven Sabbath Years.[5] Obviously the enslavement of fellow Hebrews for reasons of debt did not bring with it the terrible consequences that accompanied the enslavement of alien war captives.

This ancient world of slavery included Hellas, or classical Greece, which is considered in Chapter 1. Greek city-states varied in their dependence on slavery. In Sparta, for example, a whole class of ethnic Greeks, termed *helots*, was bound to the soil and could never become free citizens. Athens was both a cradle of political freedom and a society dependent on slavery for its economic existence. In upper-class houses slaves served as domestic servants and grew the garden crops. Far less fortunate slaves, both Greek and non-Greek alike, were worked to death in the mines, served as factory labor, and toiled on large, profit-making agricultural

---

4. Deuteronomy 20: 13–16, at https://www.biblegateway.com/passage/?search=Deuteronomy+20%3A13-15&version=NIV (accessed 17 June 2015).

5. "If any of your fellow Israelites become poor and sell themselves to you, do not make them work as slaves. They are to be treated as hired workers or temporary residents among you; they are to work for you until the Year of Jubilee. Then they and their children are to be released, and they will go back to their own clans and to the property of their ancestors. Because the Israelites are my servants, whom I brought out of Egypt, they must not be sold as slaves. Do not rule over them ruthlessly, but fear your God." Available at: https://www.biblegateway.com/passage/?search=Leviticus%2025 (accessed 17 June 2015).

estates. All of this involuntary labor allowed the freeborn, adult male citizens of Athens the leisure to debate politics and the nature of the world and to attend its festivals and games.

The earliest written records in ancient China portray a society that already had aristocrats, kings, and subordinated cultivating peasants. The peasants were bound to the land, and their position was much like slavery. These early writings, composed, of course, by the elites, recognized that the peasants produced the food they ate and the wealth that supported their relatively luxurious life. The authors also recognized that famine, flood, and war could push the peasants over the edge into rebellion. Later writings assumed slavery. The *Mozi*, for example, a philosophical text of about 400 BCE, was critical of the endemic wars of the time, which resulted in large numbers of enslaved war captives. Treatment of war captives in China sounds much like that of the early books of the Hebrew Bible. Here we read:

> The great state marshals its armies of boats and chariots to attack a blameless country. . . . The people who resist are beheaded, those who do not resist are put in bonds and brought back. The men are made drivers and grooms. The women are made grinders of corn.[6]

Testimony in the *Zhouli* (*The Rites of Zhou*) of ca. 300–200 BCE shows that Chinese authorities sent condemned criminals along with their families into slavery. According to this document:

> As for the *nu*,[7] the males enter the ranks of penal servitude, the females enter the ranks of the grinders of corn and suppliers of provisions. All those who hold rank and those who are over seventy or have not yet lost their milk teeth are not treated as *nu*.[8]

One measure of just how natural and accepted slavery was across the world is the astonishing fact that none of the founders of the world's most widespread religions and influential philosophies condemned

---

6. Quoted in E. G. Pulleybank, "The Origin and Nature of Chattel Slavery in China," *Journal of the Economic and Social History of the Orient*, 1 (1958): 188. Here "corn" is the British term for wheat and millet, not maize, which was an American cereal.
7. The extended family.
8. Quoted in Pulleybank, "Chattel Slavery," 199.

it: not the Buddha, not the writers of the Hindu sacred texts, not the authors of the Torah or of the Talmud, not Christ, not Muhammad, not Confucius or Socrates, or Plato, or Aristotle. The Hebrew and Christian portions of the Bible, for example, accept slavery as normal, and the Book of Genesis even offers a moral justification for it. Buddhism, in spite of advocating non-violence toward all living beings, lived comfortably for millennia with slaves as the main labor force for monasteries. Christ made no specific condemnation of slavery. The Apostles and the Early Church offered suggestions for alleviating the most onerous features of slavery but accepted slavery as a natural institution. Muhammad owned slaves, and Shari'a (Islamic holy law) details the just and proper treatment of slaves. Equally striking is that slavery forms part of the moral order in virtually every local religion, be it Native American, Mongolian, Scandinavian, or Polynesian.

What Was Slavery and Who Were Slaves?

Slave servitude had a variety of origins: war capture, slave raids, self-sale for debt, sale by parents for debt, birth into a slave family, and legal judgment. It is no surprise, therefore, that several kinds of slaves often existed in the same society at the same time and that the terms used to describe slavery varied even in a single language over time. In some places slaves became soldiers and army commanders, palace guards, and ship captains, while in others they served as bankers, tradesmen, teachers, trusted envoys, court officials, and concubines. Very few societies perceived any racial contrast between the slaver and the enslaved or created the large-scale plantations typical of Atlantic slavery.

This welter of terms for slavery and the variety of slave experience has generated much scholarly debate on the definition of slavery. Slavery has been described for thousands of years in too many languages, legal codes, philosophical essays, poems, and stories for simple definition. Nevertheless, across human history there have been some common features of slavery. Slavery was (and is) a *human condition*, regardless of the various ways that the person descended to that condition. A slave was generally, but not always, removed from the society of his or her birth and, therefore, had no family allies. (In Chapter 3 we will consider Barbary slavery, which, contrary to the typical cutting off of a slave's contact with his family, actually promoted such contact.) The owner generally held the slave as property (like horses or cattle) with broad control over his or her living conditions, labor, social contacts, marriage, and, in many places, children. Implied and real violence followed if the slave broke the rules. In essence, the slave's body belonged to the master.

In spite of these common features, actual slavery had great variety in practice. In some places a slave had no standing in court. In others, slaves retained some of their earnings and could buy their freedom. In yet other cases, on his deathbed a man was expected to free his slaves. No single example of slavery, therefore, whether Mediterranean, Atlantic, sub-Saharan African, Barbary, Chinese, or Russian (to name only a few of many) can be treated as *typical* slavery. At best we can accept the ubiquity of the institution and the complexity of its workings in local societies. Some broader patterns, however, have emerged from scholarship on slavery, such as the influence of far-flung legal systems. Roman law influenced slavery as far from its ancient Mediterranean roots as the colonial and post-colonial Americas, and Islamic law, affected slavery across vast regions of Afro-Eurasia.

Enslavement and Slave Trading around the World, ca. 1500

When trans-Atlantic slavery was just beginning, between 1500 and 1600 CE, there were, across the world, several long-established regions in which slaves were regularly traded. One of the most important centered on the China Sea and included Korea, Japan, China, and the major ports of Southeast Asia.

Korea had a large-scale indigenous slavery system. Government documents of the time record two hundred thousand slaves attached just to state officials. This does not include the slaves of elite families or those working for Buddhist monasteries. Plain girl slaves were simply "water fetchers," while pretty ones were trained as dancing girls.

Japan had many indigenous paths to slavery in the 1500s, which the Jesuits observed and Japanese documents corroborate: the wives and children of executed criminals were enslaved; parents and children became slaves through debt; children of slaves remained slaves; women fled abusive husbands and became slaves in great households. Especially common was slavery by kidnapping and capture in the interminable wars between noble houses. The legal system had rules for returning runaway slaves and for the status of slave children. Japanese pirates regularly seized and enslaved people who lived along China and Korea's coasts.

When the Japanese invaded Korea at the end of the sixteenth century, large numbers of Koreans were enslaved and taken to Japan. Japanese slaves and captured Koreans and Chinese were exported aboard Portuguese ships, especially to Macao.

In China several long-standing forms of indigenous slavery were common in the period 1500–1600. The courts sent the condemned and their families into exiled slavery. Destitute families sold boys into domestic service and girls into household service and as concubines. A family had the right, however, to redeem children sold during a time of financial desperation. War captives, especially steppe nomads, were routinely enslaved.

In Southeast Asia the population density was low and the scarcest resource was people. Kings, nobles, and trading elites competed to control populations through subordinate relationships, of which slavery must be considered the most onerous and permanent. The most common pathway to slavery was debt bondage. A poor man borrowed money for a wedding, funeral, or other ritual and surrendered himself when he could not repay the loan.

Successful states such as the Khmer Empire in Cambodia also had thousands of war captives, as the existing bas-reliefs at its capital show. A mid-fourteenth-century Chinese envoy to the Khmer Empire, Zhou Daguan, noted that wealthy families had upward of one hundred domestic slaves, whereas even those of modest means had ten or twenty. Most of these slaves were mountain people, whom the Khmers called *zhuangs*, or thieves, and whom they considered subhuman, thereby justifying their capture and enslavement. Once brought to the city, slaves lived in the spaces beneath the houses in which they served, the houses being built on stilts.[9]

Slaves were common in all other pre-colonial Southeast Asian cities, such as Ayudhya, Malacca, Bantaen, Acheh, and Makassar. Into this Southeast Asian world were shipped, from the east, Chinese, Japanese, and Korean slaves. From the west, slaves arrived from South India.

A second, even larger, sphere of slave activity connected India and the Indian Ocean, Persia, the Middle East, the eastern Mediterranean, Central Asia, and North and sub-Saharan Africa. Within this complex world there was both local slavery and long-distance slave trade.

---

9. Jeannette Mirsky, ed., *The Great Chinese Travelers* (New York: Pantheon Books, 1964), 214–16.

India had no large-scale plantation slavery in the period ca. 1500–1600, but slavery was common. Poor, desperate families sold girls into domestic service or as palace concubines or donated them to Hindu temples as dancing girls. Slave women were frequent gifts between rulers. Many large towns and cities had a slave market. Several thousand enslaved men and women were traded every year to the steppe peoples of Central Asia in return for horses. In North India, from roughly 1200 to 1500, traders bought and sold large numbers of enslaved men from the Middle East and Central Asia, who formed the mamluk (slave soldier) armies of the Delhi Sultanate. Some of these military slaves rose to be rulers and founded short-lived dynasties. These imports ended around 1625 with the conquest of North India by the Mughals, Central Asian descendants of Chinggis Khan, whose military structure was based on free soldiers. Military slavery, which had disappeared in North India, reappeared in the Muslim kingdoms of South India. Thousands of slaves arrived yearly from Africa, especially Ethiopia.

The Safavid Empire, which reigned over present-day Iran and adjacent regions from 1502 to 1736, had a steady demand for slaves. The shah and his nobles kept large households, which included thousands of slaves as servants, concubines, entertainers, and eunuchs. Slaves came as war captives from Central Asia and the neighboring Ottoman Empire, by purchase from India, and via a seaborne trade that also brought slaves from East Africa up the Persian Gulf and overland to Tabriz and other cities. Toward the end of the period, Turkish military slaves became an important component of the Safavid army. In addition, tribes from eastern and southern Iran raided populated areas of neighboring lands, enslaving them for field labor and to tend flocks.

The Ottoman Empire was the largest demand area for slaves in the world in the period 1500–1600. Centered on Istanbul (or Constantinople, its earlier name), the empire stretched from Baghdad in Iraq down the eastern shore of the Red Sea and included Egypt, the North African coast, Greece, current-day Bulgaria, Hungary, Albania, much of the former Yugoslavia, and the region of the Caucasus north of the Black Sea. The number of slaves flowing into the Ottoman Empire was extraordinary. At any time the sultan had a household of more than twenty thousand slaves, serving in posts that ranged from the most menial of water carriers to members of his inner circle. The same was true for all high officials, who had from five hundred to a thousand slaves in their households. Officials of the dozens of provinces had equally large households, as did wealthy traders and bureaucrats. Indeed, well-placed and wealthy slaves held their own slaves. In part it was the sequestering of women in the harem that required a large body of slaves to do the menial household work, especially carrying water, which required travel outside the house. Beyond the household there were other concentrations of slaves. The inner core of the Ottoman army consisted of approximately forty thousand military slaves, known as janissaries, the result of a systematic conscription of boys (the *devşhirme*) levied on the some Christian regions of the empire. Although slaves of the sultan, as members of an elite fighting force, janissaries were highly privileged and paid a salary. Moreover, as was true of other slave-soldier corps throughout the Islamic world, janissaries could rise to powerful civil and military positions. Such privilege and potential authority and wealth were not available to the slaves who served in the Ottoman fleet. Every naval vessel required 150 slave rowers and twenty slave riggers. The total Ottoman navy might have required eighty thousand slaves. Since many slaves—especially galley slaves who rowed these ships under brutal conditions—needed replacement every few years, it is easy to imagine a million slaves moving into the Ottoman lands every decade. Just for comparison, the annual Atlantic trade in this century was a few thousand slaves.

How, then, was this enormous demand for slaves met? Several routes brought slaves to the core of the Ottoman Empire. The largest stream for much of the period consisted of war captives from conquests of the Christian lands of Eastern Europe.[10] Military slaves came from the same areas, such as Greece and Bulgaria, but only after they had been conquered and pacified. A second stream came from the Caucasus north of the Black Sea. Competing groups had for centuries sold defeated rivals into slavery. Circassia, the small peninsula that juts down into the Black Sea, was a special case. Circassian women were famous across the Islamic world for their beauty and were routinely purchased by the sultan and elite nobles. A Circassian concubine had prospects. Any of the sultan's sons could inherit the throne, even one born of a slave woman. In fact, over the empire's long history more Ottoman sultans came from slave

---

10. In his *Turkish Letters*, which were published in 1589, the Flemish diplomat Ogier Ghiselin de Busbecq noted in his description of a convoy of Christians being transported from Hungary to the slave market of Constantinople that this was "the commonest kind of Turkish merchandise." Charles T. Forster and F. H. Blackburne Daniell, eds., *The Life and Letters of Ogier Ghiselin de Busbecq*, 2 vols. (London: Hakluyt Society, 1881), 1:37.

mothers than free wives. A third stream of slaves came from the East African coast. The Christian king of Ethiopia sold many slaves, some captured, some purchased, and the rest presented as tribute. Slave capture and sale was also typical of the remainder of the East African coast as far south as Zanzibar. Coastal slave traders had close cultural and economic ties with Arab ship captains who transported the slaves. (This trade forms the subject of Chapter 2.) The fourth stream came from sub-Saharan Africa, the result of warfare and capture. Slave caravans crossed the Sahara north to Tripoli and other major cities on the south coast of the Mediterranean.

Let us briefly consider New World slave zones in roughly the same period, ca. 1500–1600. The Inca Empire in South America marshaled vast amounts of labor, but most of it cannot be categorized as slavery. In a system of enforced labor for public projects known as the *mita*, corvée laborers served away from home for fixed periods, traveled as a group, carried their own tools, wore their traditional clothes, and served under their own leaders. Following conquest of the Inca Empire, Spanish colonial authorities continued this system of requiring villages to provide annual quotas of laborers, many of whom labored in horrifying conditions in silver mines and mercury-refining factories, but only for stipulated periods of time, normally two months, and they were paid small sums.[11] Closer to slavery were groups termed *mitmaqs*, cultivator groups forcibly removed from their lands to work on Inca-owned estates. In the absence of any written documents, scholars remain divided on how onerous and slave-like conditions were for the *mitmaqs*. Perhaps the only true slaves in the Inca Empire were a relatively small hereditary group known as *yana*, who were cultivators of elite-owned estates. Large-scale slavery in South America came as a product of European colonial conquest and exploitation. The most notorious example of this was probably the sugar plantations of Brazil on which vast numbers of slaves labored in inhumane conditions to grow, harvest, and refine a product imported from beyond the Atlantic Ocean.

In pre-Conquest Mesoamerica both the Mayan and later Aztec empires utilized slave labor on a large scale. A sixteenth-century Spanish missionary and ethnographer, Diego Durán, reported that two cities in pre-Conquest Mexico, Azcapotzalco and Itzocan, shared a monopoly

---

11. Their wages were normally half a peso per day, whereas a hired day laborer commanded between one and a half to three pesos for the same work.

on the slave trade, just as other cities enjoyed monopolies on the sale of other commodities, such as jewels and fine feathers. Some of the slaves bought and sold in these two markets were men and women, as well as boys and girls, chosen for ritual sacrifice on days sacred to the deities of Mesoamerica. Such sacrificial slaves had to be comely and "without blemish" in order to be worthy of being given to the gods.[12] Most of the market slaves, however, escaped this high honor. The vast majority of persons sacrificed in fifteenth-century Mesoamerica's continuous rituals of blood were war captives taken in "Flower Wars," whose main purpose was the capture of brave enemies worthy of sacrifice.

When brought to either of the two markets, slaves wore wooden collars about their necks, so that they could be readily identified as slaves and to hinder any attempted escape. If a slave managed to flee the boundaries of the market before being caught and then stepped into human excrement, the person was permitted to appear before officials known as "purifiers of slaves" and declare him or herself free. The authorities would then remove the former slave's fetters, strip and wash the person, and dress him or her in new clothes. From that day forward, the former slave was honored as a person of spirit.[13]

Despite the huge numbers of war captives who were sacrificed on a regular basis in rituals of appeasement to the gods, Mesoamerica's indigenous form of slavery, as was also true in South America, was in no way as disruptive and deadly as the combination of imported diseases and brutal labor conditions introduced by the Spanish colonial regime.

North of the Rio Grande River, a significant number of Indian tribes practiced slavery in one form or another but few exploited slaves on a large scale. Exceptions to that rule might have been some tribes of the Pacific Northwest, where slaves appear to have been a significant proportion of the populations of several communities. The Haida and Tlingit peoples of southeastern Alaska even engaged in the slave trade.

Slaves held by North American Indians were almost always war captives. Although some of these captives were ritually sacrificed, their relative numbers were small compared to the vast untold numbers offered in sacrifice by the various peoples of Mesoamerica. Many slaves, especially

---

12. Fray Diego Durán, *Book of the Gods and Rites and the Ancient Calendar*, trans. by Fernando Horcasitas and Dons Heyden (Norman, OK: University of Oklahoma Press, 1971), 273–80, passim.

13. Ibid, 284–86.

women and children, but also former enemy warriors, were actually integrated into the tribes of their captors through marriage or adoption. Some were also ransomed by their families or exchanged for captive members of the tribe. A few tribes also practiced debt slavery, from which the enslaved person was freed once the debt had been satisfied.

Slavery in Europe was complicated. Prior to the eleventh century it was to be found throughout the Latin West. Some cities, such as Verdun, Marseilles, and Rome, served as major slave emporia, especially for the exportation of women and castrated men to Muslim markets in Spain and elsewhere. While many Christian slave traders justified their enterprise by exclusively or largely dealing in non-Christian slaves, the pagan Vikings had no such scruples during these early medieval centuries and were heavily engaged in all aspects of the business, including capturing slaves in their raids on Christian Europe. Following their conversion to Christianity around the eleventh century, they continued in the slave trade, largely concentrating on non-Christians living along the eastern shores of the Baltic Sea. Indeed, Viking slaves, known as *thralls*, have left their imprint on the English language in the word "enthralled," which means "to be captivated" (in the sense of being fascinated by something or someone).

By the year 1500 the situation had changed, although slavery was still found throughout southern and eastern Europe, including Spain, Portugal, Italy, Poland, and Russia. Indeed, Venice and Genoa, Italy's two principal seaports, were major slave ports, and both were active in the highly profitable slave trade of the Mediterranean and Black Seas, and had been so for several centuries already.

Well, what had changed between roughly 1000 and 1500 in Christian Western Europe and why? Slavery was legal according to Roman civil law and canon (Church) law, both of which were highly popular academic subjects in Europe from the twelfth century onward. Canon lawyers, however, generally agreed that slavery was antithetical to the spirit of Christianity, and Christians could not enslave other Christians, except as a severe judicial punishment. Muslims and other non-Christians could be enslaved, especially if there was hope of their being converted to Christianity as a consequence of their servitude.

By 1500 northwest Europe was, therefore, a zone largely (but not totally) without slaves. Slavery had ceased to exist in any significant fashion in England, France, the Netherlands, and the principalities of Germany during the eleventh and twelfth centuries. Even serfdom (labor bound to a certain estate, with many additional labor obligations to the lord of the manor) had largely disappeared. The decline started earlier but accelerated with the Black Death of the fourteenth century, which made labor more scarce and valuable. Attempts by the landed aristocrats to impose more rigorous conditions were often met with peasant rebellions. Despite the rise in the value of agricultural laborers, contract agricultural labor was generally cheaper than the maintenance of serfs for a head of a manor in a developing cash-based economy, and the movement to larger, more efficient fields (enclosure) made the long, narrow strips cultivated by serfs impractical. Like their Italian and Iberian counterparts, however, traders from northwest Europe continued to buy and sell slaves, just not within northwest Europe. English and Dutch slavers grew rich on the trade. Several centuries later it was in this relatively small non-slaveholding (but slave-trading) zone of Northwest Europe that a movement for the abolition of slavery began.

The Abolition of Slavery: Successes and Failures

Only once in human history have men and women mounted a sustained moral and political movement that utterly condemned slavery and demanded its abolition in all societies. It managed to turn universal acceptance of slavery into universal condemnation in roughly 150 years (1770–1920). This enormously complicated movement has been the subject of vast amounts of scholarly study and is worthy of more.

By 1800 in England popular support was quite broad for the idea that England was a "free" country. In practice thousands of free blacks lived in England, and no slave-holder from the colonies who arrived with slaves was willing to test his rights over his slaves by publicly whipping them or using them to pay debts, a legal right taken for granted in the American colonies.

In eighteenth-century France a myth gained popularity that the country had always been free. This image of French "freedom" rested uneasily with the reality of thousands and thousands of slaves in the French plantation colonies. From the 1720s to the 1790s, a few slaves from the colonies successfully challenged their master's right to hold slaves on French soil. The courts slowly established a boundary line for slaves. There was to be no slavery in France, but slavery was legal in the colonies, such as Haiti.[14]

---

14. See Sue Peabody, *"There Are No Slaves in France": The Political Culture of Race and Slavery in the Ancien Régime* (New York: Oxford University Press, 1996).

Secular political philosophers challenged this position in pre-Revolution discussions of the inalienable rights of all people, including slaves.

In the eighteenth and the early nineteenth centuries, Europeans and American colonists could no longer ignore the slavery issue. Periodic slave rebellions in the colonies required costly military expeditions to suppress them. Slaves in the colonies fled to form independent *maroon* (escaped slave) settlements.[15] European indentured laborers in the colonies, who felt as oppressed as the slaves, occasionally joined slave rebellions, the most famous examples being the successful revolution in Haiti (1791–1804) and the doomed Nat Turner's Rebellion in Virginia (1831).

The secular and religious wings of the abolition movement lobbied, generally successfully, through the nineteenth century for a series of laws in various countries that banned first the slave trade and then slavery itself. The earliest such laws were in Denmark, England, and France, followed by other countries in Europe, including Russia. Russian conquest of the Caucasus in the 1820s largely ended its slave trade to the nearby Ottoman and Safavid empires. Later in the nineteenth century slavery was banned in the European colonies of Asia and the Caribbean. Revolutions settled the issue in South and Central America, as did the American Civil War. The last areas to ban slavery were Brazil, the princely states of India, some countries that emerged from the defeated Ottoman Empire after World War I, Ethiopia, and various kingdoms within the European-dominated colonies of sub-Saharan Africa.

Would that this sad story of human exploitation ended with the legal abolition of slavery in the first decades of the twentieth century, but, unfortunately, it did not. Slavery never fully went away, and it re-emerged with a vengeance in several forms and places in the twentieth century. Stalin's courts condemned millions to slavery in the Russian Gulag system. Hitler used slave labor in the factories of the Reich. Prison slavery was common in the American South. Millions were condemned to servitude during the Cultural Revolution in China. In our own time a phenomenon known as the "new slavery" has emerged. Slavers lure men and women with promises of high-paying foreign jobs. Instead, the victims end up without papers in hard physical work or brothels. Runaway teenagers become slaves in the sex industry. This new slavery is the subject of Chapter 4.

---

15. *Maroon* probably derives from the French *marron* or *maron*, which, in turn, is derived from the Spanish *cimmaron* (wild and untamed). Hence a *maroon* is a wild fugitive slave.

Why Do We Study Slavery?

To study slavery is not to condone it. The study of the universality of slavery is a necessary, sobering, and illustrative window into humans and their behavior—behavior that can be and has been both ethically obtuse and spiritually exalted, morally debased and morally heroic. In this light, the moral fervor of blanket opposition to slavery of the Methodists, Baptists, and Quakers of the eighteenth and nineteenth centuries must command our admiration and fuel our revulsion to slavery and our opposition to it. The *Universal Declaration of Human Rights* adopted by the United Nations after World War II must be our benchmark for upholding that most basic of human rights, the right to a life of freedom.

Chapter 1

Slavery in Ancient Athens

Athens looms large in European civilization. Two thousand years after the decline of Greek city-states, it was Athens more than any other Greek city-state that was re-discovered and celebrated in the Renaissance and during the centuries that followed.

This was a society that supported the architecture of the Parthenon by Phydias, and sculptors such as Praxiteles, that celebrated the realistic male and female nude. It supported philosophers, the most famous of whom were Socrates, Plato, and Aristotle. It patronized playwrights whose works are still read and performed: Aeschylus, Sophocles, Euripides, and Aristophanes.

Politically, Athens is famous as the first functioning democracy in the West, a rarity in the ancient Hellenic world and unknown elsewhere among the established states of antiquity. The word "democracy" derives from the Greek terms *demos* (the people) and *kratein* (to rule), thus "rule by the people." A large open assembly made decisions at which all free, adult, male citizens were able to speak. Athenians were quite conscious that they were a democracy and wrote voluminously about themselves and their government. They recorded decisions by the assembly, orations of persuasive speakers, and obituaries of their leaders. Democratic deliberations appear in their plays and their histories. A wide variety of Athenian thinkers and writers, however, also distrusted democracy.

At its peak, Athens had an army that defeated the mighty Persian army at Marathon, a navy that defeated the Persians at Salamis and subsequently ruled the eastern Mediterranean Sea, and, like other Greek city-states, colonies as far away as Italy and the Black Sea. Its distinctive black- and red-figure pottery has been excavated as far away as present-day Spain.

For all its philosophers' grand discussions of freedom, however, Athens was a society that captured and kept slaves. They were central to her economic, political, and social systems. Slavery was so "natural" to the Athenians that it was rarely discussed in the literature. It is these contradictions between freedom for some and slavery for many others that we will explore in this chapter.

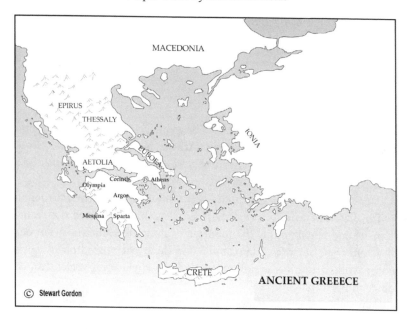

A Geographic Survey of Greece

Greece has only a handful of broad, fertile plains but is mainly a series of valleys divided by rocky hills with unproductive soil. It has the typical Mediterranean climate: hot, dry summers and a cool, rainy season that begins in November and lasts until spring. The staples of the ancient Greek economy were winter wheat, barley, lentils, and olives. Also important were the native fruits: grapes (largely for wine production), apples, figs, and pomegranates. Agricultural tools were simple: a wooden plow, hoe, and a metal sickle to cut grain. Sheep, cattle, oxen, pigs, and goats were its main domesticated farm animals. The horse was domesticated for war, travel, and sport, rather than for agricultural work. Fish were plentiful off the coasts and islands. By 1000 BCE, the chicken arrived from India.

Early Greek Slavery

From the beginning of decipherable written records in Greece, there is evidence of slavery. The first known Greek civilization, termed by modern scholars as "Mycenaean" (ca. 1580–ca. 1150 BCE), rose from humble beginnings to several regional kingdoms located in the southern peninsula known as the Peloponnesus, as well as in some areas of the northern mainland, and on some islands. Archaeologists have excavated citadels and palaces at Mycenae (hence Mycenaean civilization), Pylos, Tiryns, and Knossos (on Crete) and discovered a host of brief invoices inscribed on clay tablets in an early form of Greek known as Linear B. Some of the notations state, for example, that a slave was owned by a named group of women or that a slave followed the trade of a certain craft. One invoice notes that a man owned six hundred slaves. A group of tablets found at Pylos suggests that the listed slaves were captives (most likely the booty of piracy), an inference reinforced by the epithet "captive" following some women's names. The greater number of slaves, however, are listed as "slaves of the god or goddess." Not enough supporting evidence exists to allow us to know exactly what this means, though it is logical to infer that they were bound to temple lands.

Around 1150 BCE, Mycenaean civilization collapsed, and Greece entered what some scholars term its "dark age": sophisticated metal work, sculpture, pottery, and well-crafted furniture disappeared; writing was forgotten; trade dwindled; populations dropped significantly; and many towns and citadels disappeared. What survived were small chiefdoms based on the core Greek agricultural economy: olives, grapes, figs, wheat, barley, the local fruits, cattle, goats, sheep, and wool. In the absence of significant quantities of imported copper and tin for bronze, the smelting of local iron ore was developed mainly for weapons. A man's wealth was measured in his herds. Raiding and stealing animals and women was a way of life, as was the proper division of booty among soldiers. The great early Greek epics, the *Iliad* and the *Odyssey*, were told and re-told orally from as early as perhaps the 1200s BCE but written in the form we now know them probably between 800 and 700 BCE. They thus both recall earlier times and describe an eighth-century BCE present. Recall from the Introduction that this was roughly the same period in which the Bible's Book of Deuteronomy was probably also written down with the same assumption: the victors would kill or enslave (or perhaps hold for ransom) those defeated in war.

The *Odyssey*, the story of Odysseus' protracted return from the Trojan War to his home in Ithaca, contains many incidents showing slaves, both men and women, as a natural part of life. In Book 1 of the *Odyssey*, for example, Penelope, though still hopeful of Odysseus' return, received her various suitors as household slaves served them.

> Next a maid-servant brought water in a beautiful golden pitcher and poured it into a silver basin so they could rinse their hands; then she pulled up a gleaming table. The chief female servant of the house silently brought them bread, and various delicacies, drawing freely from the storehouse. And a carver offered plates of many different types of meats, and set them down along-side golden cups, while a male-steward, constantly walking by, poured the wine.[1]

One female slave was later assigned to the bed of each suitor.

In the world of the *Iliad* and the *Odyssey*, the best outcome of war was to return with glory, stories to tell, booty, and foreign slaves, usu-ally women. Capture meant, at best, waiting for ransom by one's family. More common and expected was death or enslavement, and the Greeks considered the latter fate to be little better than death. In the *Odyssey*, a swineherd-slave asserts that an enslaved person is very much like a dog that has lost its master: "When their masters are not around to oversee them, servants do not give a whit for the quality of their work. Far-seeing Zeus takes half the spirit out of them on the day they become slaves."[2]

The Emergence of the City-State

Around 800 BCE, Greece began to emerge from its "dark age," and much was changing. Pottery became more varied and sophisticated. Long-distance trade re-emerged, and some luxury goods re-appeared. By 750 BCE, Greece had entered a phase that modern scholars term the Ionian Renaissance. The population of Hellas rose, and the self-governing city-state known as a *polis* (plural *poleis*) emerged as a distinctive political structure. It is, however, important to remember that much of Greece,

---

1. ΟΔΥΣΣΕΙΑΣ Α (book 1), ll. 143–47, trans. A. J. Andrea from the Greek text of W. Walter Merry and James Ridell (eds.), *Homer's Odyssey, Volume I, Books I–XII*, 2nd rev. ed. (Oxford, UK: Clarendon, 1886), 16. Copyright © A. J. Andrea, 2016. All rights reserved.
2. ΟΔΥΣΣΕΙΑΣ Ρ (book 17), ll. 321–23, trans. A. J. Andrea from the Greek text of D. B. Monro (ed.), *Homer's Odyssey, Volume II* (Oxford, UK: Clarendon, 1901), 111. Copyright © A. J. Andrea, 2016. All rights reserved.

especially in the north, did not go through this political transformation and remained divided into chiefdoms and even independent villages.

The new city-states were, above all, the product of a rising aristocracy, which owned large agricultural estates but also lived in the city. These aristocrats succeeded in substantially decreasing the relative power of the local chieftain, and officials and a council took over many of the functions previously performed by the chief and his court. Despite their role in breaking the power of the local chieftains, the aristocracy's authority did not go unchallenged in many of the emerging poleis. All Greek city-states struggled with the question of who was a citizen and who, therefore, could be present and speak in the council. Moreover, armies in these city-states were no longer recruited on a kinship basis, as they had been in the *Iliad* and the *Odyssey*, but consisted of loyal citizens. This meant that the benefits of citizenship could not be limited to the aristocracy.

War between the various city-states was endemic but with some limitations. Citizens of any city-state, mainly farmers, had to be convinced that war was the right path. Debates over war are some of the most detailed documents we have from ancient Greece. If primary loyalty was to one's city-state, it is also true that a league, or combination, of city-states to advance common political and military aims was also a typical arrangement. These sorts of coalitions recurred throughout ancient Greek history. It is important to remember that these leagues not only mobilized forces but typically forbade attack by any state on any other signatory state, thereby decreasing local war and destruction. These leagues often did not last more than a generation, suggesting both ongoing tension in the internal politics of each city-state and the changing relative power of city-states within the league.

To free up enough labor to administer the city-state and staff armies was a continuing political problem. To have enough rowers to have naval pretensions meant that an even larger portion of the citizens had to serve. Slavery was a common solution to this problem. Slaves labored in the fields and workshops, worked the mines, and rowed the galleys.

City-states varied both in size and in their commitment to trained armies and expansion by war, but none was more military-centered than Sparta, the great power of southern Greece below the isthmus, a region known as the Peloponnesus. The state was organized so that every male citizen was a trained soldier and none performed agricultural work. Instead, a class known as *helots*, who were mainly Greek war captives re-settled on Spartan agricultural estates, performed all such work.

Helots were probably closer to serfs (that is, bound to the land) than slaves (bought and sold as a commodity), but they held a special low status, which was enforced by periodic Spartan violence against them. They reciprocated with periodic rebellions, sometimes allying with Sparta's enemies.

Athens as a City-State

Written sources on Athens as it emerged as a city-state are particularly meager but suggest that at the end of the "dark age" it participated in the generally rising population and the process of incorporation of the city and surrounding villages into a single political unit. Athens was quite successful, when compared to other Greek states, at engendering a sense that the surrounding villages were as much "Athens" as the city itself. This integration was done without subjugating the rural population as Sparta had done. Athens thus had no angry and restive helot population. As in other city-states, a regulated government with defined offices replaced the former chiefdom. In one famous incident in 632 BCE, Kylon, a member of a powerful landed family, tried to take over the government, thereby becoming a *tyrant*, which in Hellenic political terms simply meant a person who illegally seized power over a state. The attempt was foiled when farmer-soldiers surrounded the Parthenon, where the usurper fled. The incident demonstrates the emerging commitment to Athens as a political idea and resistance to a return to rule by kings. Shortly after this incident, Draco gave Athens its first set of written laws, which defined homicide as a state offence to be adjudicated by courts, rather than simply an occasion for a blood feud. The payment of recompense, settled by the state rather than blood feud, meant that productive members of society stayed alive and that families could participate together in civic functions.

More important for the long-term success of Athens were the laws of Solon (ca. 600 BCE), an aristocrat deemed wise enough to tailor laws for the city-state's circumstances. Solon identified the core issue as that of citizenship, which was the means through which to maintain loyalty to and participation in the city-state by all levels of society. One central problem was the impoverishment of small farmers. Aristocratic control of the best land allowed them to hire marginal small farmers. If small farmers failed and went into debt, aristocrats could loan them the money they needed and effectively enslave them, a practice, as we have seen, known as debt-bondage. How could small farmers be full loyal citizens when more and more ended up as sharecroppers on the large estates of aristocrats? Solon, therefore, abolished debt-bondage. Another of Solon's remedies was to divide society into four categories: the elite whose land produced five hundred bushels of produce or more, those with enough wealth to keep a horse (and serve as cavalry), those whose wealth consisted of a pair of oxen (and served as well-trained, heavily armored infantry known as *hoplites*), and the poor (who served as auxiliaries). He gave duties to each level, restricting powerful offices to men of the top category and lower offices to the middling two ranks. The poor could, however, fully participate in the assembly. Solon correctly foresaw that balancing the greed and privilege of the aristocrats against the leveling instincts of the poor would be the core political conflict of Athens for the next two centuries. This political tension was played out in discussions in the councils, in the writings of philosophers, in dramas composed by the city's great playwrights, and in court cases.

The predominant viewpoint was that Athens' citizens should be "masterless," that is, not bound by either long-term employment contracts or long-term obligations to an aristocratic family. The Athenian ideal was that citizens should own enough land to live on its proceeds. There was also a consensus that each Athenian citizen should serve in the army or navy and as a magistrate and juror at least a few times in his life. The aristocratic viewpoint found landed income to be the only honorable wealth. Some philosophers, such as Aristotle, held all physical labor in contempt. Far less worthy, in this aristocratic view, was a citizen who owned an urban workshop, business, or bank, or taught for a living. Even less worthy were the poor, who were citizens by birth but had no means of a regular income. The struggles between the lower orders and the aristocracy seesawed back and forth. One of the important factors in the gradual increase in political influence of the lower orders was the need for rowers in the galleys. Expanding Athenian power meant more ships and more rowers. Without poor citizens to row, the expansion was stymied. This very real military need swayed power to the lower orders and resulted in the expansion of privileges, eventually resulting in democracy and making Athens something of a rarity in the Hellenic world. Although all free Greek males throughout the Hellenic world considered themselves responsible citizens of their native city, the vast majority of city-states, such as Sparta, were ruled by small groups of elites known as oligarchs.

With the poor going off to row and the small farmers legally insulated from debt-bondage, how was a landed aristocrat to find the labor to cultivate his estates, or the entrepreneur to find workers and artisans for his factory as Athenian exports of high-quality manufactured goods, especially painted pottery vessels, rose dramatically? Slavery was the answer. As the Athenian empire expanded, its military successes produced an increasing number of slaves through war capture. Many ended up on the estates of the rich, but they were everywhere in society: teachers, business agents, artisans, laborers, concubines, and ship captains and sailors.

The Legacy of Athenian Slavery

Athens' dominance as a political and military power ended with its defeat in the protracted Peloponnesian War with Sparta (431–404 BCE) and its eventual conquest by Macedonia in 338 BCE. Culturally, however, its influence remained enormous for many more centuries. Roman elite sons were sent to Athens for proper training in rhetoric and philosophy. After the decline of Rome (ca. 200–400 CE), Greek learning largely disappeared from the emerging civilization of Western Europe. It carried on, however, elsewhere, first in the Byzantine Empire and then under the Muslim caliphate of Baghdad and, farther west, Muslim Al-Andalus (current-day Spain and Portugal) and Sicily. In the twelfth century, the legacy of Greece began to re-enter Europe from Muslim Spain via translations from Arabic. Over the next few centuries, increasing numbers of Greek books (and Arabic commentaries upon them) were translated in Western Europe, first into Latin and later into Europe's various vernacular languages.

By about the year 1600, enough books had been translated that it was obvious that slaves and slave labor had been present in Athens. Was it possible that this presumed "cradle of liberty," this society that wrote with so much pride of the freedom of its citizens and its democracy, actually had an economy dependent on slave labor? For conservative thinkers watching the rise of democratic ideas in the eighteenth century, just before the revolutions in America and France, the answer was obvious. Athenian democracy could not have functioned without slaves to do all the necessary work while citizens idled away their time in self-government. Athenian democracy consisted of an "idle mob" and the slaves who supported it. For conservative, anti-democratic writers, such as Montesquieu, the fall of democratic Athens to oligarchic Sparta in 404 BCE was inevitable, the result of its rotten foundation on slavery.

For all subsequent political writers, Athenian slavery was a fact that could not be wished away. Some, such as Marx, sought to explain slavery as a phase in the inevitable development of human society and economy. Athens, being early in human history, was based on slavery, just as it should have been. Other writers and researchers settled into a centuries-long discussion over just how many slaves there were in Athens and what proportion of the population slaves formed. Was Athens a society in which slaves greatly outnumbered citizens, or was Athens basically a peasant society of small farmers to which were added some slaves, the number much smaller than the free citizens?

Modern Scholarship

Three centuries into this discussion of Athenian slavery, scholars have arrived at a few points of consensus:

1. To Athenians, slavery was a natural part of life around them. It went deep into their past, as evidenced by frequent references to enslavement and slaves in the earliest Greek epics, such as the *Iliad* and the *Odyssey*. None of ancient Greece's famous philosophers wrote a book or even a chapter entitled "On Slavery." The ideal societies envisioned by Socrates, Plato, and Aristotle did not condemn slavery or preclude slaves. Later philosophers, such as the Stoics, the Epicureans, and the Skeptics, all assumed slavery to be a natural social element. The Athenian philosophers generally framed the concept of freedom in opposition to long-term subordination to an employer or to political subservience to a monarch, not in opposition to slavery. They did not criticize democracy as specifically associated with slavery nor did they see it as a system that was antithetical to slavery.

2. The general inattention to slaves in Athenian writing and inscriptions makes the sources on slavery rather threadbare. Extant written records that reflect the realities of slavery are always about something else: a court case about destruction of sacred trees or a failed mining venture; naval recruitment lists; or a handbook on

In Greek and later Roman comic plays, slaves were often presented as conniving and dishonest individuals. Here a ceramic statuette, which dates to ca. 400–330 BCE and was crafted in the Greek region of Boetia, depicts an actor portraying a slave sitting on an altar, which is an act of sacrilege, and rummaging through a purse he has just stolen. (CC-BY-SA 3.0 license.)

how to run a farm. Slaves appear in documents as part of a property settlement or a description of a household. They were stock characters, sometimes humorous, sometimes intelligent and thoughtful, in tragic and comic plays. Domestic slaves were occasionally portrayed on Greek painted vases, though the numbers of such portrayals is small in comparison to other themes, such as war, athletics, religious festivals, and the gods.

3. Throughout the writings about Greek slavery, there is no consistent and uniform term for a slave and only a slave. The terms used to describe slaves were borrowed from other relations in Athenian society. *Doulos*, for example, can mean a slave, but it also referred to any relationship of dominance and possession, such as submission to an outside military force or even the forces of nature. Another common term for a slave is *oiketes*, but this term also refers to any servant who did tasks for a family (*oikos*). *Andropoda* (man-footed beast) normally referred to the unluckiest of war captives. As was the case with the roughly seven thousand Athenian warriors and their allies who were captured at the Sicilian-Greek city of Syracuse in 413, the andropoda was condemned to become a two-footed beast of burden, as opposed to a *tetrapoda*, or four-footed animal.

4. It must be emphasized that slavery was not equally practiced by all Greek city-states. Some states, such as Sparta, used more slaves than Athens per person, and some states used virtually none. Military victory sometimes meant executing the defeated men and enslaving the women and children, such as Athens did to Melos in 416/415, but not always. Sparta, for example, did not require enslaving the conquered population of Athens after its victory in the Peloponnesian War.

Recent research on Athens and its slavery has moved away from the writings of Athenian philosophers on how society ought to work to more concrete considerations of how it actually worked. Broadly, research on Athenian slavery has followed one of two approaches. The first is sociological, which seeks to compare many societies and find which characteristics of societies correlate with slavery. This approach has resulted in some useful work in showing that simple economic analysis cannot explain why slavery appeared in one locale and not in another. For example, it has been widely assumed that slavery was a simple result of an abundance of land and too few people to cultivate it. Thus, the only way to create wealth was to control people, and slavery was a "natural" product of this process. Comparative historical-sociological research into slavery in many societies demolishes this hypothesis. There was little or no correlation between slavery and societies that had large amounts of land and few people. The comparative sociological approach has uncovered unexpected factors that affect the presence of slavery in societies, such as the effect on slavery of women working in agriculture outside the house. The sociological approach has, however, been justly criticized on a number of points. The primary data for what is treated as "typical" of a society usually come from a single report by an anthropologist, historian, or bureaucrat, written at a single moment in history. Making this single observation into the "typical" pattern of the society does not allow for change over time or even the possibility of misperception of the local situation by the single observer. Comparing distant societies also blurs differences in the actual local practice of slavery and the subtleties of local language in describing it.

The second modern approach to understanding Athenian slavery has been purely historical, attempting to understand slavery as it actually worked in various periods of Athenian history. This research has involved careful reconsideration of the standard sources and examination of some new material, such as inscriptions.

The picture of Athens that emerges from these newer studies has important implications for understanding its slavery. Citizenship in Athens was complex and exclusionary. It was a narrow and closed society, not the open, liberal, and egalitarian one we might expect from its practice of democracy. A man (women, by gender, were not citizens) to be a citizen, especially onwards from the Age of Pericles (461–ca. 430), had to be born into a recognized local community, known as a *deme*. Names often reflected that of a famous ancestor of the group. *Demes* ran their own finances and festivals and gathered to talk about political issues and military situations. Every future citizen as a small boy was introduced into another corporate group, known as a *phratry* (brotherhood), which consisted of a much wider group of more distant kin. At eighteen the young man entered military service in the company of a *tribe*, another corporate group that included men of various *demes*. He would fight and possibly die with the comrades of the *tribe* with whom he served. Some of the apparently endless round of religious ceremonies and processions in Athens were organized according to *demes* and *phratries*. Other religious events consciously mixed these groups. They all, however, reinforced the self-image and self-importance of citizens.

Religious ceremony, political participation, and military service all reinforced who could and who could not be an Athenian citizen. Women, children, Athenian men who never served in the army or navy, and resident foreigners (*metics*) played no part in Athenian democracy or other political affairs. Women born of a free, native-born mother and a citizen father had limited rights but were not considered citizens. None of these groups could normally offer evidence in court cases. The line between citizens and slaves was even more absolute. Athenian law assumed that a slave, if his testimony were absolutely necessary, would testify truthfully only under torture, though there are no cases in the record of actual torture of slaves to elicit testimony. Freed slaves had no opportunity to become citizens, no matter whom they married or if they worked their way to wealth. Slaves and ex-slaves, along with women and foreigners, were thus outside the code of honor expected of Athenian men, as members of tribes, *phratries*, and *demes*, and as citizens.

Slaves in Athenian society were unevenly distributed. The lowest economic level of Athenian citizens consisted of the poor who lived on a meager government stipend. They, of course, had no slaves. Neither did

Fourth-century BCE Athenian grave stele of Iostrate examining a jewel box that her slave maid servant has brought her. Royal Ontario Museum.

the next lowest echelon of Athenian citizens, perhaps a third of the citizen population, who lived by family labor on a subsistence-level small farm or in the city as ordinary teachers, artists, doctors, or owners of small workshops.

Slaves were common among middle- and upper-class urban households. Slave men and women did much of the drudgework: cooking, carrying water, laundry, and cleaning. The numbers were not large. Even the wealthiest houses probably had a dozen or fewer household slaves. The top two thousand families, however, also owned skilled artisan slaves: shoemakers, shield makers, potters, knife makers, and the like. These slaves served in workshops of their owners or were leased to others' workshops. Their wages constituted a regular source of income for wealthy families.

In the countryside outside Athens, poorer farmers had to make do with family labor. More prosperous small family farms could afford perhaps a single slave who served as a general farmhand but could also be leased to a nearby farmer once the owner's plowing or harvesting was completed. Large estates owned by wealthy Athenians, however, typically depended on the labor of a hundred to a thousand slaves to produce bulk wine or olive oil for export.

The largest concentration of slaves in the area around Athens was in the silver mines. Wealthy Athenian investors formed speculative co-ventures to lease slaves and excavate a portion of the silver-bearing site. Current scholarly opinion suggests that at least ten thousand and possibly as many as twenty thousand slaves regularly worked in the silver mines. Their lives were miserable and short, with no chance of manumission.[3]

The city's war galleys, central to the Athenian transformation of former allies into client states, had mixed slave and citizen rowers. Athenian writers were justly proud of citizens who served in this extraordinarily hard and dangerous work, which originally had served as the impetus for granting Athens' poorest citizens full participation in the *polis'* political life. Nevertheless, the reality was that slaves filled the naval benches of Athens' enemies and eventually also manned the galleys of Athens. Athenian writers were so reticent to speak of slave rowers that we have only chance and scrappy information, but a modern scholar has suggested that

---

3. A technical term, derived from the Latin "to let go from one's hand" or "to release from control," which is used exclusively to denote the freeing of a slave, usually in some formal manner and often as a gratuitous act by the master.

slaves constituted 20 to 40 percent of the rowers on Athenian warships. The tradition of slave rowers on Mediterranean galleys lasted for more than two thousand years, finally ending, as we shall see in Chapter 3, only in the 1700s.

Athens: A Slave Society?

Scholars have asked whether classical Athens was a "slave society" or merely a "society that owned slaves." What is at issue is how much slavery was at the center of the economic and social system and how much it affected relationships of people in the society. Was wealth predicated on and measured in ownership of slaves? Was there a predictable supply of slaves, and were they a major part of the society's trade? Was there a credit system that supported slave ownership? Was the government involved in supplying slaves and regulating slave markets? Were a high percentage of all workers slaves? Did the state and other institutions depend on the labor of slaves for its income? Were slaves prominent in virtually all aspects of the culture?

By these measures Athens was somewhere in the middle, neither fulfilling all of the criteria for a "slave society" nor being merely a "society that kept slaves." Slaves were certainly central to several sectors of the economy. They were the sole labor force on large estates and in the mines. And the silver mines provided the means for building the fleet that was critical in the war with Persia and upon which Athens based its dominance over its "allies" in the powerful Delian League (ca. 477–404). Slaves provided much of the labor for urban workshops and some of the labor on the more prosperous small farms. As an act of civic service, citizens also regularly sent slaves to row ships of the Athenian fleet. Several Athenian upper-class philosophers wrote that physical labor was only suitable for slaves and beneath the dignity of a citizen.

This degree of slaveholding does not, however, seem to meet all the criteria for a "slave society." There is no evidence of slave breeding as a conscious policy, just as there is no evidence that the Athenian government maintained slave markets. Unlike "slave societies," slaves were not the sole or chief measure of a man's wealth. Land, goods, workshops, and urban houses were all considered wealth. The state had little bureaucracy at the time, but it had no particular economic motive to promote slavery and did not use slaves in such institutions as it had. Religious institutions did hold some slaves, but they also regularly received donations from the various corporate institutions of free citizens. The trade of Athens was not primarily in slaves. Its olive oil, wine, and pottery circulated throughout much of the Mediterranean world. In Athens many besides slaves worked. Small farmers cultivated their land. The more prosperous small farmers worked alongside the single slave who served as a farmhand. Free artisans, such as stonemasons, worked side by side with slaves in construction, though some evidence suggests that free craftsmen were generally more skilled than their slave counterparts. Free sculptors, woodcarvers, pottery painters, shoemakers, artists, doctors, and teachers lived by the income of their own work.

Life as an Athenian Slave

Let us shift the viewpoint from owners and economics to that of Athenian slaves. Many came from capture in wars between Hellenic city-states, but they also came from lands far beyond Greece. One list includes slaves from Malta, the Black Sea region, Syria, Scythia (the region north of the Caspian Sea), Lydia (in present-day Turkey), and Thrace (in what is today northern Greece and Turkey in the direction of Istanbul). Slaves such as these would have been "barbarians," that is, speaking little Greek when they arrived in Athens. It is unlikely that they remained with members of their family with whom they might have been captured. The work was endless. Slaves had no days off for the religious festivals that their masters attended. Children of slave women, regardless of the father, had no hope of becoming citizens. At best they might be freed with their mother. Slaves could legally be beaten and tortured by private owners and public officials without notice or comment. Many escaped when they could in response to Athenian defeats by Sparta during the Peloponnesian War.

Perhaps the only mitigating factor of slavery in Athens was the possibility of being freed by a master. The data are fragmentary but suggest a good number of freedmen resided in Athens. For example, for a brief period in the later fourth century BCE, the Athenian government assembled lists of the slaves freed in each year. The records give the name of the freed slave, his or her occupation, and the owner's name and place of residence. Freed slaves tended to stay in or around Athens, finding work that matched their skills. In one group of wills, freedom was granted to approximately one-third of each man's slaves. None of the lists of freed slaves includes a single slave from the mines, who served for life—a generally short and miserable life.

Why, then, did Athens opt for slavery? At the broadest level, warfare made slaves available at a price that the middle and upper reaches of Athenian society could afford. There were no moral or philosophical strictures against owning slaves. Certain profitable activities available to the upper classes, especially large agricultural estates and the silver mines, needed steady intensive labor that slaves provided. All of this does not explain, however, why Athenians bought slaves for these jobs rather than hiring local labor.

Robin Osborne has argued that slavery was attractive to Athenians as much because of political ideology as because of economics. Local labor was simply unavailable to do drudge household work, long-term agricultural work, and labor in the mines because Athenians widely believed that such work was not suitable for freeborn citizens. Athenian democracy rested on a belief that all citizens were more or less equal. Some were richer and some poorer, but none "owned" another through long-term contract or employment. This situation gave them an equal voice in the assembly, in military obligations, and before the law. Slave labor may not have been necessary, as eighteenth-century critics of Athenian democracy thought, to create the idle leisure to make democratic debate possible. It is likely, however, that slave labor was essential in creating conditions that made it seem as if every citizen was, at least nominally, equal.

Osborne's argument does not, however, address a larger and more important issue. Which came first, the availability of slaves or Athenian beliefs in the unsuitability for a citizen of long-term subservient work? The issue is far larger than the case of slavery in Athens. While Osborne's analysis might explain Athenian slavery as a development within Athenian history, it surely does not explain slavery in the myriad societies, including the vast majority of Greek states that did not have democracy. As we shall explore in subsequent chapters, slavery, that is the ownership and full exploitation of another human being, acquired many different political, economic, and moral justifications over its long and sordid history. None of these justifications was the "cause" of slavery. Moral justifications followed the availability of slaves, which could be used to better the lives of their exploiters.

Sources: Athenians Speak about Slavery

Plato on Slavery

As a philosopher, Plato (428–348 BCE) considered both the ideal and
the actual. In his writings he often discussed the actions and attributes
of the ideal man, how an ideal city might be governed, or what the ideal
laws might be. Plato was well aware, however, that his Athenian (and
Greek) world differed substantially from the ideal world that he con-
ceptualized. These contradictions were at the center of many of his dialogues. The following excerpts are taken respectively from *The Laws*,
which centers on the nature of law and lawmaking, and the dialogue
known as *Lysis*, which revolves around the issue of friendship. In the
first excerpt, an unnamed Athenian stranger, a Spartan called Megillos and a Cretan named Cleinias discuss slavery. In the second excerpt,
Socrates, the main character in most of Plato's dialogues, recounts his
teasing of Lysis.

Questions for Consideration

In daily life, as Plato describes it, what were the consequences of slavery?
What, according to Plato, was the slave master's first duty? Why? Who
was Plato's presumed audience in the second excerpt, and how might this
dialogue affect their self-image? What do these two excerpts allow us to
infer about slavery in fourth-century Athens?

✦✦✦✦✦

How to Treat Slaves[4]

Athenian. In the next place, we have to consider what sort of property
    will be most convenient. There is no difficulty either in understand-
    ing or acquiring most kinds of property, but there is great difficulty
    in what relates to slaves. And the reason is that we speak about

---

4. Plato, *Laws*, trans. Benjamin Jowett, part 3, 18–21, accessed January 16, 2011, http://
www.ellopos.net/elpenor/greek-texts/ancient-greece/plato/plato-laws-3.asp?pg=18.

them in a way which is right and which is not right; for what we say about our slaves is consistent and also inconsistent with our practice about them. . . .

We know that all would agree that we should have the best and most attached slaves whom we can get. For many a man has found his slaves better in every way than brethren or sons, and many times they have saved the lives and property of their masters and their whole house—such tales are well known.

Megillos. To be sure.

Ath. But may we not also say that the soul of the slave is utterly corrupt, and that no man of sense ought to *trust* them? And the wisest of our poets, speaking of Zeus, says:—

Far-seeing Zeus takes away half the understanding of men whom the day of slavery subdues.[5]

—Different persons have got these two different notions of slaves in their minds—some of them utterly distrust their servants, and, as if they were wild beasts, chastise them with goads and whips, and make their souls three times, or rather many times, as slavish as they were before;—and others do just the opposite.

Meg. True.

Cleinias. Then what are we to do in our own country, Stranger, seeing that there are such differences in the treatment of slaves by their owners?

Ath. Well, Cleinias, there can be no doubt that man is a troublesome animal, and therefore he is not very manageable, nor likely to become so, when you attempt to introduce the necessary division, slave, and freeman, and master.

Cle. That is obvious.

Ath. He[6] is a troublesome piece of goods, as has been often shown by the frequent revolts of the Messenians, and the great mischiefs which happen in states having many slaves who speak the same language, and the numerous robberies and lawless life of the

---

5. A quotation from the *Odyssey*. See above for a slightly different translation of this ambiguous sentence.
6. A slave.

Italian banditti, as they are called.[7] A man who considers all this is fairly at a loss. Two remedies alone remain to us—not to have the slaves of the same country, nor if possible, speaking the same language; in this way they will more easily be held in subjection: secondly, we should tend them carefully, not only out of regard to them, but yet more out of respect to ourselves. And the right treatment of slaves is to behave properly to them, and to do to them, if possible, even more justice than to those who are our equals; for he who naturally and genuinely reverences justice, and hates injustice, is discovered in his dealings with any class of men to whom he can easily be unjust. And he who in regard to the natures and actions of his slaves is undefiled by impiety and injustice, will best sow the seeds of virtue in them; and this may be truly said of every master, and tyrant, and of every other having authority in relation to his inferiors. Slaves ought to be punished as they deserve, and not admonished as if they were freemen, which will only make them conceited. The language used to a servant ought always to be that of a command, and we ought not to jest with them, whether they are males or females—this is a foolish way which many people have of setting up their slaves, and making the life of servitude more disagreeable both for them and for their masters.

✦✦✦✦✦

Slaves as Masters[8]

What do you mean? I said. Do they[9] want you to be happy, and yet hinder you from doing what you like? For example, if you want

---

7. Plato refers here to two separate phenomena. The first reference is to the centuries-long wars and revolts on the part of the Messenian Greeks against the Spartans. The Messenians had been reduced to *helot* status in the eighth century BCE, but they remained a constant irritant to their Spartan masters. The second reference is to bandits in Italy and Sicily, presumably escaped slaves. Plato traveled on three occasions to various Greek states in Italy and Sicily.

8. *Lysis; or, Friendship in Dialogues of Plato*, translated into English with analysis and introductions by Benjamin Jowett (New York: Scribner, Armstrong, 1873), 46, accessed January 16, 2011 at http://www.ellopos.net/elpenor/greek-texts/ancient-greece/plato/plato-lysis.asp.

9. His parents.

to mount one of your father's chariots, and take the reins at a race, they will not allow you to do so—they will prevent you?

Certainly, he said, they will not allow me to do so.

Whom then will they allow?

There is a charioteer, whom my father pays for driving.[10]

And do they trust a hireling more than you? and may he do what he likes with the horses? and do they pay him for this?

They do.

But I dare say that you may take the whip and guide the mule-cart if you like;—they will permit that?

Permit me! indeed they will not.

Then, I said, may no one use the whip to the mules?

Yes, he said, the muleteer.

And is he a slave or a free man?

A slave, he said.

And do they esteem a slave of more value than you who are their son? And do they entrust their property to him rather than to you? and allow him to do what he likes, when they prohibit you? Answer me now: Are you your own master, or do they not even allow that?

Nay, he said; of course they do not allow it.

Then you have a master?

Yes, my tutor; there he is.

And is he a slave?

To be sure; he is our slave, he replied.

Surely, I said, this is a strange thing, that a free man should be governed by a slave.

✦ ✦ ✦ ✦ ✦

---

10. Charioteers were professional athletes who competed at the sacred games, such as the Olympic Games.

Aristotle on Slavery

The treating of the captured as booty to be enslaved had not changed from the time of the *Iliad* and *Odyssey*. Aristotle (384–322 BCE) was Plato's student and one of Athens' greatest writers on philosophy, logic, natural science, rhetoric, theater, and politics. All his training under Plato suggested that the various groups in society—the rulers, soldiers, and producers—were essentially different from each other. There need not be a means by which a person could rise in rank since he would be unsuited to belong to that rank. Aristotle was, however, an excellent observer of the world around him and realized that this Platonic ideal did not necessarily correlate with the world in which he lived. Here he considers two opposing opinions of his time. The first is that both the body and the soul of a slave differ from that of a free man. The slave is, therefore, a slave by nature and can never aspire to be a free man. The contrary view was based on the observation that on the battlefield a man could in the same day pass from a free and honored soldier to being a slave. How, then, could his essential nature be different from one hour to the next?

Questions for Consideration

What does this discussion suggest about stability or flux in personal identities at the time? According to Aristotle, what role do nature and the soul have in this process? What roles do accident and chance play in enslaving a person? What are the distinctions between a citizen and a barbarian? What would have been Aristotle's response to the statement in Plato's *Laws* that "the soul of the slave is utterly corrupt."

◆◆◆◆◆

Aristotle's *Politics*[11]

[A man] is a slave by nature; and that man who is the property of another, is his mere chattel, though he continues a man; but a chattel is an instrument for use. . . .

---

11. Aristotle, *The Politics of Aristotle; or, a Treatise on Government*, trans. William Ellis, intro. by A. D. Lindsay (London: J. M. Dent, 1912), book 1, chaps. 5, 6, 7.

[I]t is the intention of nature to make the bodies of slaves and freemen different from each other, that the one should be robust for their necessary purposes, the others erect, useless indeed for what slaves are employed in, but fit for civil life, which is divided into the duties of war and peace; though these rules do not always take place, for slaves have sometimes the bodies of freemen, sometimes the souls; if then it is evident that if some bodies are as much more excellent than others as the statues of the gods excel the human form, every one will allow that the inferior ought to be slaves to the superior; and if this is true with respect to the body, it is still juster to determine in the same manner, when we consider the soul; though it is not so easy to perceive the beauty of the soul as it is of the body. Since then some men are slaves by nature, and others are freemen, it is clear that where slavery is advantageous to any one, then it is just to make him a slave.

But it is not difficult to perceive that those who maintain the contrary opinion have some reason on their side; . . . whatsoever is taken in battle is adjudged to be the property of the conquerors: but many persons who are conversant in law call in question this pretended right . . . for victory is always owing to a superiority in some advantageous circumstances; so that it seems that force never prevails but in consequence of great abilities. But still the dispute concerning the justice of it remains; . . . for it may happen that the principle upon which the wars were commenced is unjust; moreover no one will say that a man who is unworthily in slavery is therefore a slave; for if so, men of the noblest families might happen to be slaves, and the descendants of slaves, if they should chance to be taken prisoners in war and sold: to avoid this difficulty they say that such persons should not be called slaves, but barbarians only should; but when they say this, they do nothing more than inquire who is a slave by nature, which was what we at first said; for we must acknowledge that there are some persons who, wherever they are, must necessarily be slaves, but others in no situation; thus also it is with those of noble descent: it is not only in their own country that they are esteemed as such, but everywhere, but the barbarians are respected on this account at home only; as if nobility and freedom were of two sorts, the one universal, the other not so.

✦✦✦✦✦

The Life of a Courtesan-Slave

This legal case was brought by an Athenian citizen named Apollodorus against another named Stephanos around 340 BCE. Based on internal evidence we think that Stephanos was in his late fifties or early sixties at the time and Apollodorus might have been around fifty. Only the oration by Apollodorus before the jury remains, not the rebuttal by Stephanos or the verdict. The accused was Neaira, Stephanos' long-term lover and concubine. Apollodorus' speech was long thought to be by Demosthenes (384–322 BCE), Athens' most famous orator, but modern scholarship makes Apollodorus the author of the piece.

Why did Apollodorus initiate this case? Eight years earlier he and Stephanos had been on opposite sides of a serious political faction fight over how to finance Athens' ongoing war against Phillip of Macedon. Stephanos had tried, through the courts, to bankrupt and discredit Apollodorus so that he and his children would have lost not only all their assets but also citizenship in Athens. Penniless, they would have had to go into exile. Apollodorus prevailed in this case but sought revenge against Stephanos. The case against Neaira presented an opportunity to discredit Stephanos, remove his and his children's citizenship, and break him financially. The case probably also reflects political conflict at the time, but not enough documentation remains for scholars to reconstruct the factions and the issues.

The case hinges on strict Athenian citizenship laws. About a century before the case, Athens tightened the citizenship laws by excluding children born of an Athenian citizen father and a foreign woman. Only two ways remained for a person to claim Athenian citizenship: being born of Athenian parents or being honored with citizenship for some exceptional service to Athens, especially during wartime. Apollodorus accused Stephanos of taking a foreign slave woman as a wife, having three sons and a daughter with her, and passing them off as Athenians. To do so was a serious crime against the state. Punishment was banishment and financial ruin. In Athenian practice at the time, however, there were various ways that a man who was a citizen could game the system so that his illegitimate male progeny would be recognized as citizens and his daughters accepted as native-born free women worthy of marrying an Athenian citizen. These tactics involved, for example, relatives swearing that the man was married to a free, native-born woman and that the child was hers.

One of the ironies of the case is that Apollodorus was himself the son of a freed male slave, who had acquired Athenian citizenship and married an Athenian woman. His father had prospered in business and owned a bank. On his death, the bank and his widow passed to another freed slave who had also acquired Athenian citizenship.

Although there is no extant record of the trial's outcome, modern scholars have judged Apollodorus' case relatively weak. His rambling argument acknowledges that Stephanos had always claimed that his four children were not by Neaira but by another woman, a free, native-born Athenian. Stephanos' three sons were already in their late twenties at the time of the case and had been examined and fully accepted as Athenian citizens with the attendant duties, group memberships, and privileges. Apollodorus ignores the sons and focuses on the daughter, named Phano, accusing her of being the daughter of Neaira and, therefore, falsely enjoying the status of being free and native born. She, however, had married an Athenian citizen who—even after divorce—acknowledged their son as his heir and formally introduced him into citizenship.

Highly paid and sought-after courtesans were denied citizenship, but they were probably the freest women in the city. They were educated and rich, kept luxurious independent houses, hosted salons and parties, and moved at will through the city. Wives, in contrast, had arranged marriages with the proper ceremonies, rights to inherit from their original family, legal protections, and much authority in the sphere of house and family. Wealthier wives were more secluded in their houses, but poorer citizen women worked outside the house as wet nurses, vegetable sellers, or weavers. Only in special circumstances was the testimony of any woman accepted in court or assembly.

The career of a high-end, desirable courtesan was relatively short. If she was a slave, the owner took her earnings and gifts, and she probably ended up as a common prostitute. A few courtesans found long-term lovers and became concubines of rich men. This was the situation of Neaira. She and Stephanos seem to have loved each other and shared a house for years. She raised the four children even if they were not her own. Neaira would have been in her fifties at the time of the accusations.

The paraphrase below is from Apollodorus' digression on Neaira's life as a foreign slave and prostitute, none of which was in dispute. What is fascinating for us, millennia later, is his inadvertent description of the complicated network of clients, the movement from one city-state to another, and the possibilities of buying one's way to freedom.

Questions for Consideration

What course did Neaira's life take? What could have motivated Timanoridas and Eukrates to offer Neaira a price for her freedom that was
far less than what they had paid for her? How much initiative does the
argument attribute to Neaira? What do your answers to these two questions suggest about the status, limitations on, and opportunities open
to this sort of slave? How was the truth of the testimony of a slave to be
established in the Athenian legal system?

❖❖❖❖❖

Apollodorus, *Against Neaira*[12]

Apollodorus began by telling the court that a freedwoman named
Nikarete bought Neaira and six other pretty girls at a young age,
trained them, and brought them up to be prostitutes, passing
them off as her daughters. The seven girls commanded high prices and were much in demand. Eventually she sold all seven girls.

Neaira was purchased for thirty minas by two young patrons,
named Timanoridas and Eukrates, and kept as their prostitute
and slave.[13] When both young men were about to get married,
they offered Neaira her freedom, for a price. They offered her
only a thousand drachmas toward a total price of twenty minas
(two thousand drachmas); they demanded Neaira contact former patrons, and indeed, she raised the money to buy her own
freedom. One patron, named Phrynion, took the money that
former patrons had given Neaira and added enough of his own
money to buy her and set her up as prostitute in Megara.

---

12. A paraphrase of Apollodorus, *Against Neaira*, ed. and trans. Konstantine A. Kapparis
(Berlin: De Gruyer, 1999), 16.
13. At this time a mina equaled one hundred silver drachmas. Athenian jurors received
a daily subsidy of three bronze obols (half of a drachma), which was considered sufficient to provide a poor family of three with bare, day-to-day subsistence. *Hoplites* (heavy-
armored infantry soldiers) and skilled workers earned, on average, one drachma daily.
Three thousand drachmas, therefore, would maintain a small, poor family for more than
sixteen years.

In the two years Neaira worked as a prostitute in Megara, she met Stephanos, the accused in the suit. She wanted to live in Athens, since she found the men of Megara poor and cheap, but was afraid of Phyrion, whom she had robbed. Stephanos—according to Appolodorus' oration—guaranteed her safety and brought her to Athens. To ensure her status, he would treat her as his wife, introduce her three children as his own, and when they were old enough introduce them into his phratry and make them citizens.

Apollodorus accused Stephanos of the illegal act of presenting Neaira's children as his own, thereby due all the rights of an Athenian citizen. He demanded that Neaira's slaves be put to torture to reveal whether the children were, as Stephanos claimed, those of an Athenian citizen, or were, in fact, Neaira's. Above all, Apollodorus asserted that Neaira was no wife and her children could not be citizens. According to him,

> We have courtesans for pleasure, concubines for the daily needs of our body, and wives to beget us legitimate children and to be trustworthy guardians of our households.

✦✦✦✦✦

Slaves on Agricultural Estates

The following excerpts are from the *Oeconomicus* (*The Household*), a treatise on the proper management of agricultural estates composed by Xenophon (ca. 430–ca. 354 BCE). Born into at least the equestrian class in Athens, he had a privileged upbringing, was familiar with Platonic-style dialogues, and was a student of Socrates. He served in the cavalry during the last years of the Peloponnesian War (431–404) and wrote the history of the war's final seven years. Later he served as a mercenary with Cyrus the Younger in the prince's unsuccessful struggle to seize the throne of Persia. Despite his Athenian citizenship, Xenophon preferred the oligarchic politics and military culture of Sparta. There is no scholarly consensus on when Xenophon wrote the *Oeconomicus*, but it is clear that he had direct knowledge of agriculture and estates. In the following sections, Xenophon puts the dialogue into the mouths of Socrates and Ischomachus, an expert on estate management.

Questions for Consideration

How did owners and slaves on estates depend on each other? How close was the daily proximity of slaves and owners? How would Aristotle's argument that slaves were "different-by-nature" hold up in the rural estate setting described by Xenophon? When referring to the slave who supervised his household, what did Xenophon mean by "the just live richer and freer lives than the unjust"? Does this dialogue suggest in any way that slaves might have had some control over their condition? If so, how did masters work to define and limit that "freedom"? How idealized do the descriptions seem? How did you arrive at your answer to this question?

◆◆◆◆◆

The Duties of a Wife on an Estate[14]

"'Indeed,' ... I said,[15] 'your duty will be to remain indoors and send out those slaves whose work is outdoors, and oversee those who are to work indoors and to receive whatever is brought in and to distribute as much of it as needs to be given out.[16] And you must be careful and safeguard whatever is put into storage so that you do not expend in a month what was meant to last a year. And when wool is brought to you, you must see that cloaks are made for those who desire them. And you must see to it that dried grain is in good condition and eatable. One of your duties, however, might perhaps seem to you rather thankless. You will have to see to it that any slave who is ill is cared for.'"

14. ΟΙΚΟΝΟΜΙΚΟΣ, Xenophon, *Memorabilia and Oeconomicus*, ed. E. C. Merrchant, trans. A. J. Andrea (London: William Heinemann, 1923), VII, 35–37 (pp. 424–26), copyright © 2016.
15. Ischomachus is relating to Socrates a conversation he had with his wife.
16. Here he refers mainly to produce that is brought in and stored as opposed to cash.

"'Oh, no' cried my wife, 'it will be most pleasing because they who are well cared for will be grateful and more loyal than before.'"

Slaves on the Estate[17]

"I showed her[18] that the entire house faces south, obviously so that it is sunny in winter and shaded in summer. I showed her the women's quarters as well, separated by a bolted door from the men's, so that nothing might be removed that should not be, and so that slaves might not breed without our permission. As it is, honest slaves generally are more loyal if they have a family; dishonest slaves, however, are all the more prone to mischief if they are married."

Equipment Used by Slaves[19]

"Once we had organized our moveables by category, we placed everything in its proper place. After that, we showed the slaves who have to use them where to place the utensils they use every day—for baking, cooking, spinning and so forth. And we handed these over to their care and told them to keep them safe and sound."

Selecting, Training, and Motivating Slaves

A. The Housekeeper[20]

"When it came to appointing a housekeeper, we chose the woman whom we judged to be most moderate in eating, drinking wine, and sleeping, and who is exceedingly modest with men. She is the one also who seemed to have the best memory and possesses the forethought to avoid punishment

---

17. ΟΙΚΟΝΟΜΙΚΟΣ, IX, 5 (p. 440).
18. Ischomachus' wife.
19. ΟΙΚΟΝΟΜΙΚΟΣ, IX, 8–9 (pp. 440–42).
20. Ibid., IX, 11–13 (p. 442).

through her negligence and to consider how, by pleasing us in some way, she might be rewarded by us in return. We also taught her to be loyal to us by sharing with her our joy when we were happy, and when we were troubled inviting her confidence. Moreover, we trained her to be zealous when it comes to improving our estate by becoming thoroughly familiar with its operation and allowing her to share in its prosperity. Furthermore, we inspired in her a sense of justice by honoring more the just than the unjust, and showing her that the just live richer and freer lives than the unjust. We then installed her in her position of authority."

B. The Overseers[21]

"I venture to say that many matters must now claim your attention. . . ."[22]

"I assure you, Socrates, I am not neglecting the matters to which you refer. I have overseers in the fields."

"And when you need an overseer,[23] Ischomachus, do you search about for a man who is skilled in the position and try to purchase him . . . or do you train your overseers yourself?"

"'By Zeus,[24] Socrates,' he replied, 'I try to train them myself. For if someone must be capable of taking charge when I am absent, what else does he need to know except that which I know myself? If I have the ability to manage the various types of work, I can certainly teach someone else what I know.'"

"'Then,' I said, 'the first requirement is that he is loyal to you and your household if he is to represent you in your absence.

---

21. Ibid., XII, 2–16, passim (pp. 462–68).

22. Socrates begins this part of the conversation by apologizing for keeping Ischomachus from other duties.

23. The overseer was a slave in charge of other slaves who worked outside the house on the estate's lands. Another name for him would be foreman.

24. The chief Greek god.

If an overseer is not loyal, of what use is the knowledge that he might possess?'"

"'None, by Zeus,' said Ischomachus. 'But loyalty toward me and my household is the first lesson that I try to teach.'"

"And just how, by the gods, do you teach this man whom you have chosen to be loyal to you and your household?"

"'By Zeus,' said Ischomachus, 'by rewarding him whenever the gods bestow on us some good thing in abundance.'"

"'You mean to say,' I asked, 'that they who enjoy a share of your blessings are loyal to you and want to do good by you in return?'"

"Yes, Socrates. I find that this is the best way of securing loyalty."

"'Well, Ischomachus, let us suppose he is loyal to you,' I said. 'Is that sufficient to make him a competent overseer?'" . . .

"'Well, by Zeus,' replied Ischomachus, 'when I want to make men of that sort overseers, I teach them diligence.'"

"'By the gods,' I asked, 'how so? I thought that diligence is something that can in no way be taught.'"

"True, Socrates. It is not possible to teach diligence to every single person one encounters." . . .

[*Ischomachus and Socrates now discuss the types of persons who are unteachable—drunkards, the lazy, and the overly passionate love smitten.*]

"'What then about they who are passionate for gain?' I asked. 'Are they also incapable of being trained to be diligent regarding farm work?'"

"'Not at all, by Zeus,' said Ischomachus. 'In fact, they can be easily led to be diligent in such matters. It simply suffices to point out to them that diligence is profitable.'"

"'What about the others,' I asked, 'who are self-controlled regarding the vices you condemn and are moderately desirous of profit? How do you train them to be diligent in the way that you want them to be?'"

"'It is simple, Socrates. Whenever I see that they are diligent, I commend them and try to show them honor. Whenever they appear negligent, I try to say and do the sort of things that will sting them.'"

C. Teaching Obedience[25]

"'Well, now, Socrates, other creatures learn to be obedient in two ways: by punishment whenever they disobey and by reward when they are eager to serve you. . . .'"
[*Ischomachus now gives the examples of how colts and puppies are trained.*]

"People can be made more obedient simply by talking with them and demonstrating the advantages of obedience. In dealing with slaves, however, the type of training found suitable for wild animals is likewise an effective means of teaching obedience. You can accomplish a lot with them by filling their bellies with the food that they desire. They who are ambitious are motivated by praise, for some personalities are as hungry for praise as others are for food and drink. Now these things that I do with the aim of making more obedient people for my service I also teach to those whom I wish to appoint as my overseers. And I furthermore assist them in the following ways. For the clothing and the sandals that I must supply for my workers are not identical. Some are better than others and some are of inferior quality. By this means I can reward the better slave with the better articles and give the inferior articles to the less deserving. 'For, Socrates,' he said, 'it seems to me that good workers become discouraged when they see that they have done all the work but that those slaves who are unwilling to work hard or run risks as needed receive the same as they. As far as I am concerned, the better and worse workers should not receive the same treatment. When I know that the overseers have distributed the best articles to the most deserving workers, I commend them. But if I see that flattery or some other favor has won one special treatment, I do not overlook it. Rather, Socrates, I reprimand the overseer and try to teach him that favoritism benefits no one, not even himself.'"

---

25. ΟΙΚΟΝΟΜΙΚΟΣ, XIII, 6–12 (pp. 472–74).

Chapter 2

East African Slavery

The East African slave route, which existed for approximately two thousand years, was characterized by multiple sources of slaves, a variety of traders and destinations, and marked differences in slaves' life experiences. Throughout the vast Indian Ocean region, slave trade and ownership were considered completely moral and legal, regardless of the religion of the slaver or the buyer.

To begin consideration of the East African slave trade, let the reader imagine a triangle with all sides equal. The top point rests on Baghdad. The western leg passes south through Mecca, the Red Sea, the Horn of Africa, and down the African coast to the island of Zanzibar opposite the mainland of current-day Tanzania. The eastern leg begins at Baghdad, passes down the Euphrates River through the Red Sea and the Indian Ocean, ending on the west coast of India. The base of the triangle connects India directly across the Indian Ocean to Africa (see map). Commodities, ideas, flora and fauna, cuisine, diseases, language, and slaves passed along all three legs of this triangle. Curries, tropical medicines, and plants, such as the banana, moved from India to Africa. Various sects of Islam passed out of the Middle East along both the African and Indian legs of the route. Spices from Malabar (the southwestern coast of India) or farther east were crucial to the economies and cultures of the Middle East. Many trading families, including Muslims, Jews, and Hindus, had representatives in ports and cities along the legs of this triangle.

The East African Slave Route in Roman Times

The earliest record of the East African slave route is a book entitled *The Periplus of the Erythraean Sea* (now known as the Indian Ocean), written around 50 CE by a Greek ship captain as a guide for other traders. Its title is literally translated as "Sailing around the Red Sea," and for the ancient Greeks the "Red Sea" included the Persian Gulf and Indian Ocean, as well as the present-day Red Sea.

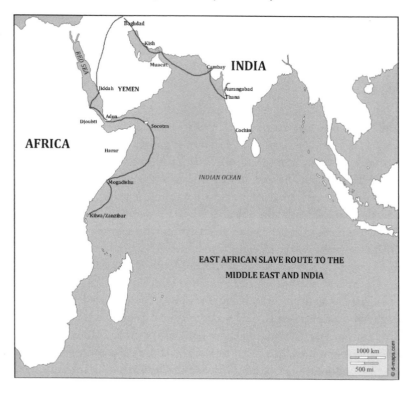

True to its name, this short, no-nonsense text described relevant features of the Red Sea, the east coast of Africa as far south as Zanzibar, and the oceanic voyage east to the coasts of India. It listed ports, sailing instructions, and products that could be profitably imported and exported. The *Periplus* got the basics of the East African trade route quite right. The timing of the route was critical. Monsoon winds of June through August favored sailing north on the western coast of India as well as north on the eastern coast of Africa. Winter winds reversed, favoring sailing south along the coasts of Africa and India (see map). This yearly wind pattern meant that a transit from South India or Africa to a Middle Eastern port, such as Aden at the mouth of the Red Sea, might take only a few weeks, but the return trip would be delayed for months. Ship captains were generally unwilling to risk the light and variable winds outside the pronounced monsoon wind pattern and, therefore, made only one round-trip per year.

The *Periplus* recommended that traders bring to the African coast a variety of fabrics and manufactured goods: Egyptian linen cloth, Indian colored cloth, cloaks, pottery, several sorts of glassware, copper for cooking pots and ornaments, and (in spite of indigenous African iron production) iron for spears, axes, adzes, and swords. To compete successfully with traders from India and the Arabian Peninsula, the author of the *Periplus* knew that traders from the Mediterranean needed particular types of Indian cloth that Africans expected, such as a luxurious fabric known as mallow-cloth, belts, and several kinds of specialty cotton whose characteristics are now unknown. Traders could buy these items at large ports such as Mauza (later Mocha) at the mouth of the Red Sea. In trade for these items, the book recommended acquiring tortoiseshell and rhinoceros horn, but especially East African slaves.

The *Periplus* rightly listed East African slaves with other luxury goods. In Rome, East African slaves were never a source of inexpensive drudge labor. The Roman Empire acquired plenty of such slaves for galleys, estates, and household labor largely from its conquests throughout the Mediterranean and beyond but also through purchase in numerous active slave markets throughout the empire. East African slaves, in contrast, were expensive and exotic showpieces in the retinues of rich men. The Roman visual record (sculpture, painted vessels, and frescoes) shows black Africans as jugglers, musicians, wrestlers, cupbearers, and riders of exotic animals in processions. One of Cleopatra's closest handmaidens, for example, was a black African.

In Roman literature, all African slaves were termed "Ethiopians" and characterized by not only their blackness and their wooly hair but also their extreme height or their extreme shortness. Such comments suggest that the African slaves were not in fact from Ethiopia (then the empire of Axum, located on a high plateau inland from the Horn of Africa) but were captured by Ethiopian slavers from several groups, including people from the plains to the west of Ethiopia. Slaves had traveled from Ethiopia down the Nile since early Dynastic Egypt (ca. 3000 BCE). Many tomb and temple paintings of the subsequent centuries feature war captives from upriver marching off to slavery. The route was never easy. A vast swamp, known as the Sudd, separates the upper river toward Sudan and Ethiopia from the lower river of ancient and modern Egypt. Navigating its shifting vegetation-choked channels required brutal work and considerable local knowledge. Once south of the Sudd, a slaver either hired a boat to run the various cataracts on the upper river, navigable only in the summer months, or marched his charges across hundreds of miles of desert to join the Nile farther downstream.

In the Roman centuries, Italy was not the only destination for slaves from East Africa. Some went to Egypt, and others went to the estates and cities of the Roman Empire, located in what are now Turkey, Spain, and the Middle East. Overall, the number of East African slaves shipped was probably not large. A few thousand per year might be a reasonable guess. In the Mediterranean West, the demand for such slaves probably declined along with the political and economic decline of the western portions of the Roman Empire after roughly 300 CE.

The eastern half of the Roman Empire continued on as the Byzantine Empire long after the decline of Rome itself. Constantinople was its prosperous, luxurious, and well-defended capital. The Byzantine Empire's social and political arrangements remained profoundly Roman. It appears that slaves worked in many of the urban workshops and on estates, just as they had in the western Roman Empire. The rights of masters and some basic protections for slaves were set forth in the Theodosian Code (438) and the Code of Justinian (529–534), both being compendiums of legal precedent and rulings by Roman emperors. The legal situation for a slave was grim. If, for example, he informed against his master, the sentence was death.[1]

It must be emphasized, however, that scholars know little about where and how the legal code was enforced. Evidence for the experience of slaves in the Byzantine Empire largely consists of a handful of documents, several of doubtful authenticity, and a few wills that belong to later centuries. Historians will, therefore, never know exactly how important most slaves were to the Byzantine Empire or their actual conditions of life. The source of most slaves was as war captives from the margins of the Byzantine Empire, such as Persia and the Caucasus. Modern scholars have speculated that the retinues of the rich, both at their estates and townhouses, probably included a few exotic African slaves.

Documents of somewhat more detail exist regarding eunuch slaves, that is, castrated boys and men, who were generally war captives. Eunuch slaves, who served as palace and household guardians,[2] court officials,

---

1. The Church made some attempts to ameliorate the condition of slaves, especially Christian slaves. Church leaders, for example, pronounced that marriages between Christian slaves were fully recognized by the Church, even if permission from the master to marry was still required.

2. The name means in Greek "alone in bed," which refers to the eunuch's emasculation. They were further known in Greek as "keepers of the bed chamber," a reference to eunuchs' role as trusted guardians of the female quarters in a house—trusted because it was presumed they would not be sexual predators.

entertainers, and sex partners, were common across Afro-Eurasia, including such cultures as ancient Sumer, Egypt, and Assyria, China, Persia, Rome, India, Korea, and the Ottoman Empire. In the case of Byzantium, eunuch slaves were well integrated into the upper levels of society, including the imperial court, the Church, the army, the civil bureaucracy, and the homes of elites. Despite this integration, eunuchs were regarded as belonging to a third gender—neither male nor female. A ninth-century Byzantine treatise lists seventeen official positions that were reserved exclusively for eunuchs, the theory being that, because they had no children or other family, they would not harbor divided loyalties. At the turn of the tenth century, however, eunuchs were allowed to adopt children to whom they could pass on their accumulated wealth and offices. Several of Byzantium's most notable generals were eunuchs. Castrati, noted for their sweet, pure voices, served in choirs throughout the empire and beyond. Eunuch slaves were also highly valued as diplomatic and wedding gifts. Due to these career opportunities, there are recorded instances of some free men offering either themselves or their sons for castration. What percentage of slaves survived the horrifying process of castration is anyone's guess.[3]

Slavery in Early Islam

By the mid-seventh century, the Byzantine Empire could not avoid the rise of the new religious, political, and military movement known as Islam. Coming out of the desert and caravan cities of the Arabian Peninsula, the movement was based on tough tribal fighters. In accounts of the earliest battles, Islamic forces mocked their opponents, the Qurashi, Muhammad's own clan in the Mecca area, for "recruiting blacks with massive shoulders."[4] A few African slave soldiers were even identified by name. The flag bearer on the Qurashi side at the Battle of Uhud was an Ethiopian named Su'ab. The Islamic writers derided the Qurashi's choice of standard-bearer.

---

3. The seventh-century Byzantine physician Paul of Aegina described the process of castration in his *Medical Compendium in Seven Books*, but he provided no data regarding survival rates.
4. Abdul-Faraj al-Isfahani (897–967), *Kitab al-Aghani* (Book of Songs) (Bulaq, Egypt, 1868), 1:20.

> You boasted of your flag
> The worst [grounds for] for boasting
> Is a flag handed over to Su'ab.
> You have made a slave your boast,
> The most miserable creature that walks the earth.[5]

Another Ethiopian slave soldier named Washi fought for the Qurashi in
the same battle and later transferred his allegiance to the Muslims. These
two African slave fighters were hardly alone during the early Islamic wars.
One source, describing the Battle of Badr of 624, states that the Ethiopians attacked, throwing their lances. According to early Islamic tradition, Bilal, a slave of Ethiopian descent, was purchased by Muhammad's
closest friend (and father-in-law), Abu Bakr, and freed upon becoming
a Muslim. He accompanied Muhammad to Medina, where he served
as the community's first *muezzin*, calling the faithful to prayer five times
daily. He is mentioned as a significant figure in some early sayings of
the prophet. Scattered references show Africans participating in all the
Islamic factional battles of the period 640–680.

African soldiers are mentioned in many campaigns, for example, the
conquest of Egypt (640–641). The following interchange is between a
conquered administrator in Egypt and the commander of the Islamic
troops, who was half African and half Arab.

> "Remove this black from my presence and bring someone else
> to speak with me." [The Muslims] answered together, "He is
> the best of us, the most learned, and the wisest. He is our lead-
> er (*sayyid*), he is the most virtuous, and the most admired. We
> all pay attention to what he says and to his views. The *amir*[6]
> ordered that we obey him and he ordered that we not contra-
> dict his views or his speech." [The *Muqawqas*][7] asked, "How
> do you feel about this black being the best among you when he
> should be the most debased?" They answered: "By no means!
> Even if he is black (as you see he is), he is the best of us in
> rank, in precedence, in intelligence, and in wisdom. Blackness

---

5. Ibn Hisham (d. 834?), *As-Sira an Nabawiya* (The Life of the Prophet) (Cairo, 1955),
2:78.
6. Commander.
7. Egyptian commander.

is not something we reject." The Muqawqas said to 'Ubada, "Advance, black man, and speak gently to me, for I am in dread of your blackness; if you speak severely, it will increase my dread." 'Ubada advanced toward him and said, "I have heard your speech. Among those I command are a thousand men, all of them black, every one of them blacker than I and yet more hideous to look at. If you saw them, you would dread them excessively."[8]

This source and several others suggest that many African soldiers were not slaves but free Africans living in the Arabian Peninsula at the time. The references are, however, too meager to establish whether these Africans were freed slaves or had emigrated from Africa. That free soldiers were somehow recruited from Africa also cannot be ruled out.

Islamic armies quickly conquered Palestine, Syria, the eastern half of Anatolia (present-day Asian Turkey), the provinces east of the Black Sea, and Armenia, in addition to Afghanistan, Persia, Egypt, North Africa, and most of Spain.[9] Scholars have speculated that during this time of rapid Islamic conquests, the number of African slaves declined simply because slaves captured in war cost nothing and were available in large numbers. The rapid expansion of Islam ended by 750 CE, and the glut of war-captured slaves ended.

The enormous new Islamic empire was ruled first from Damascus in Syria from 660 to 750 and then from its new capital at Baghdad, beginning in 762, but it was subject to constant fissures, ethnic and factional conflict, regional breakaway kingdoms, and outright rebellion. Soon after the Abbasids (750–1258) overthrew the previous dynasty of caliphs, documents record a slave army belonging to the new dynasty, which consisted of four thousand African slave soldiers stationed at Mosul (in present-day Iraq).[10] This tantalizing reference gives no context of how this army

---

8. Ibn 'Abd al-Hakam (803–871), *Futuh Misr wa Akhbarha* (Conquest of Egypt and Some Account of It [Egypt]), ed. C. C. Torrey (New Haven, CT: Yale University Press, 1922), 66.

9. Fred Donner, *The Early Islamic Conquests* (Princeton, NJ: Princeton University Press, 1981), remains the best source for this period of Islamic history. There was much slave-taking at the time. Christian histories of martyrs recount the Persian capture of Jerusalem and the enslavement of its population in 614 CE.

10. Al-Tabari (839–923), *Tarikh al-usul wal-Muluk* (History of the Prophets and Kings), ed. M. J. Goeje et al. (Leiden, Netherlands, 1879–1901), 3:305.

got there, what it was doing there, or what happened to it. There had been earlier African forces, such as 'Uhada's in Egypt, but we know of none other on this scale before this period.

The notion of a slave army might seem exotic, even impossible. Why would a slave fight for his master? The fact is that kings and other leaders in many cultures bought slave soldiers for a common reason. Many of them remembered all too vividly that the first order of their reign was war against competing claimants to the throne, generally members of their own family. They, therefore, sought a fighting force of utter and complete loyalty, unsullied by crosscutting attachments of family, religion, ethnicity, faction, or language. If their master instructed them to fight, they fought. They insured their lord against violent coups. As we have seen, military slavery appeared early in the Middle East and was a persistent feature for more than a thousand years.

By the year 800, the core of the caliph of Baghdad's army consisted of military slaves, who were known as *mamluks* (owned persons). The scale of the caliph's slave army was what was new, numbering in the tens of thousands. Few of these were, however, Africans. The caliph's new slave army was composed primarily of Central Asian tribesmen, mainly Turks from the steppes. These would, over the centuries, evolve into the Mamluk rulers of Egypt, Syria, and northern India and the feared janissary corps of the Ottoman Empire. None of these later elite slaves was African.

From this admittedly scrappy evidence we can say only a few things for certain about slavery on the East African coast between the first-century *Periplus of the Erythraean Sea* and, say, 800, when the armies of the Islamic Caliphate no longer had large African contingents. First, texts record African slaves in a wide variety of places: Egypt, Mecca and Medina, Baghdad, and Basra. Second, most of the references are to African soldiers rather than household slaves or field laborers. Third, the evidence of slave origins suggests a trade only from the northern portion of the East African coast, the same as during Roman times, namely, the well-populated plains west and south of the highlands of Ethiopia. Ethiopia appears central to this slave trade. Finally, no concrete evidence of slaving farther south, say below Mogadishu, appears in the extensive geographies produced under the Caliphate of Baghdad, though they routinely discussed both the character of peoples and trade items for the region.

The Zanj Revolt

One of the few incidents of the early Islamic world that focused on African slaves was the Zanj Revolt of 870–885. Our main source for the Zanj Revolt is the historian and theologian al-Tabari, who at the time lived in Baghdad and received news of the Zanj campaign. The term "Zanj" appears in early Islamic geographies, and scholars at first thought it referred to a particular place, such as the East African coast below Mogadishu. Modern scholars, however, find that the term probably meant black Africans generally, regardless of their ethnicity or origin. The word itself is likely Persian, rather than Arabic, and translates as "rust colored," distinctively different from the lighter skin color of Persians.[11]

The background to the revolt features a financially strapped caliph of Baghdad bestowing large areas of marshland upstream from the mouth of the Euphrates (near present-day Basra in Iraq) to his nobles for plantation development. Male slaves were purchased to drain the fields, difficult work under brutal conditions.

The leader of the revolt came from a mixed background. His grandmother had been a slave from India. He grew up poor but free, traveling to Bahrain, Baghdad, and Basra. His radical Islamic preaching denied the authority, secular or religious, of the caliphs of Baghdad, for which he was expelled from Basra in 868, only to return the following year when there was armed conflict between the two Turkish regiments that protected the city. He redirected his preaching to slaves clearing the nearby marshes, presenting himself as a *mahdi*, or savior, whose mission was to better the lot of slaves and replace the corrupt rulers in Baghdad with a just and holy rule. He adopted the slogan of earlier Islamic rebels; the most qualified man should rule, even if he were an Ethiopian slave. His preaching quickly widened the revolt's base to include like-minded nomads from the nearby desert, sedentary Arabs from the marshes, and urban artisans.

The revolt rapidly drove out managers and troops from the new marshland estates. The Zanj army then attacked up and down the Tigris and Euphrates rivers, consistently defeating caliphate armies sent to subdue the rebels. By 871 the major city of Abadan in the Tigris Delta surrendered, and the caliphate's principle port of Basra had been sacked by the Zanj infantry and hired Arab cavalry. The Zanj attacked a flotilla of merchant

---

11. Dan Shapira, "Zoroastrian Sources on Black People," *Arabica* 49 (2002): 117–22.

boats, killed the fighters on board, captured slaves, and seized the goods. Cities and towns paid taxes to the Zanj. According to al-Tabari, "When the city of Abbadan surrendered to the Zanj army they seized all the slaves and weapons found there."[12] The commander recruited the "Abbadanian" slaves to his own Zanj troops. The women of the town were sold into slavery. The population of the city of al-Ahwaz in present-day Iran fled at the Zanj approach, except for one Ibrahim ibn Mudabbir who was in charge of taxes and estates. The Zanj defeated his troops and captured all his money and slaves. Season after season the revolt grew, the Bedouins of the marshlands offering safe haven for the Zanj and their allies. At their height, the Zanj armies are estimated to have included nearly one hundred thousand field slaves and freed urban slaves. For more than a decade the Zanj held off the caliphate's armies and retained control of the lower Tigris and Euphrates Rivers. On one occasion they fought their way to the walls of Baghdad. Contemporary observers estimated the casualties from that battle at more than ten thousand. In spite of several military expeditions, Baghdad was unable to reestablish control over the Basra region until 879. The rebels' last stronghold was taken three years later.

Modern scholars' careful analysis gives the slaves many origins, but mainly Ethiopia, Sudan, and its immediate neighbors. The slave trade, if this interpretation holds up to further research, was large in numbers but concentrated in geographic scope and did not include the more southerly coast of East Africa. It is important to note that the Zanj Revolt was both a political movement that sought to replace the caliphate with a new power and a religious-social movement that attempted to better the lot of the exploited. It was not a movement against slavery as an institution. The Zanj rebels, in fact, sold captives into slavery. Abolishing slavery is perhaps too much to expect from a movement that recognized the authority of the Qur'an, with its explicit acceptance and regulation of slavery. Indeed, the earliest codes of Islamic law and commentaries upon them also established rules governing enslavement and the treatment of slaves.

Ethiopia and Its Slave Trade

Slavery can be documented early in Ethiopia's history. The following inscription comes from Axum, the ancient capital of Ethiopia. It

---

12. Al-Tabari, *Tarikh*, 3:307.

is undated but likely third century CE. The pattern this inscription describes was typical of many societies at the time. The contemporary late Roman Empire, the Sassanian Empire (centered in modern-day Iraq and Iran), and the tribes of the Arabian Peninsula also turned war captives into slaves.

> So we took the field against him [the enemy], ... and we sent out our army, and they killed him, made prisoners and [took] booty. And we slaughtered down Sani and Tsawanto and Gema, and Zahtan, four nations, and we took prisoners, Alita, with both his sons. And the number of the slaughtered men of A[dan] amounted to 503, and the women 202, total 705. Prisoners of men and women of the camp followers, men 40, and women and children 165, total 205. Booty of oxen 31,900 and small cattle about 80,000. And he returned back safe with the people of [Adan], and raised up the throne here in Sada.[13]

For the millennium after the Zanj Revolt (880–1880) the populated region that today includes Sudan, Uganda, and Kenya remained a remarkably consistent source of supply of slaves. The slavers were from Ethiopia and the plains of what is today Somalia. The main markets also remained remarkably stable: Cairo, Constantinople (later called Istanbul), Baghdad, and various other cities in the Middle East, including Damascus and Aleppo. Ethiopia's first legal code, the Fetha Nagast, or Law of Kings, produced around 1240, recognized slaves as central to the economy and defined the acquisition and holding of slaves as the natural order of things. In fact, the Ethiopians, as Christians, quoted directly from the biblical Pentateuch for their moral justification for slavery. The legal code also attempted to define the proper relations between slaveholder and slave, acknowledging a tangled web of sex and service. A few of the legal strictures were, as follows:

> [Liberty] is in accord with the law of reason, for all men share liberty on the basis of natural law. But war and the strength of horses bring some to the service of others, because the law of

---

13. J. Theodore Bent, *The Sacred City of the Ethiopians, Being a Record of Travel and Research in Abyssinia in 1893*, translation and commentary by D. H. Müller (London: Longmans, Green, 1893), 260–61.

war and of victory makes the vanquished slaves of the victors. Mosaic Law shows that unbelievers and their children must be held as slaves since it is written there: "Those whom you take from the people who dwell around you and the aliens who dwell among you, let them, men and women, be your slaves. You shall buy [slaves] from among them and from among their offspring born in your land, and they shall be for you and your children after you, as an inheritance."[14]

The sale of a believing [Christian] slave to an unbeliever is not allowed. The children of a slave belong to their master, be they born from a free woman or from a female slave. The child of a female slave belongs to her master, whether he is born from a free man or from a slave and regardless whether he was born from a union by marriage or from fornication with someone other than her master. In case she becomes free during her pregnancy, the child in her womb is free, because the mother was freed while she was carrying him in her womb. One may set free the child in the womb without setting free the one who is pregnant. The child of a once-free woman born from a free father or from a slave who was manumitted [is free], even if she became a slave after she conceived him and before she gave birth to him, because the enslavement of another must not affect one's state of freedom.[15]

Father Francisco Alvarez, the first papal ambassador to the king of Ethiopia, resided at the capital and traveled the kingdom's roads from 1520 to 1527. His memoir notes that Ethiopia at the time was a full slave society. Male slaves provided the labor for tilling the fields and harvesting the grain on estates owned by the king, his nobles, and the many churches. Slave women did the washing, cleaning, and cooking in noble houses. Several outlying provinces on the western fringes of the Ethiopian highlands paid tribute to this Christian state in slaves. The king of Ethiopia regularly sent out shipments of slaves for sale.

Father Francisco described the caravans of slaves from the interior highlands of Ethiopia to the coast:

---

14. Leviticus 25:46.

15. *The Fetha Nagast: The Law of the Kings*, trans. Abba Paulos Tzadua, ed. Peter L. Strauss (Addis Ababa, Ethiopia: Faculty of Law, 1968), 175.

No one passes here by road except in a cafila [caravan] which they call a *negada*. This assemblage passes twice a week, once in coming and another time in going, or to express it better, one goes and the other comes; and there always pass a thousand persons and upwards, with a captain of the *negadas*, who awaits them in certain places.[16]

If his observation on the size of slave caravans is even close to correct, it suggests an enormous slave trade at the time. A caravan of a thousand slaves every week works out to roughly fifty thousand per year or a half a million slaves every decade.

Slaves were also captured south of the medieval Ethiopian state. Each year slave raiders set out from the Muslim-held eastern lowlands of what is today Ethiopia, raided south into what is today Kenya and Uganda, and returned to a bustling port named Zayla, which was located on the coastal desert of Somalia. Most of these slaves were sent to Baghdad, but some were shipped directly east to India. Pieter van den Broeke, a Dutch trader, was on the coast of Yemen in 1616 and observed two boats arriving from Zayla. Together they had 240 male and female slaves. Indian merchants readily bought the lot for export to the west coast of India.

Malik Amber (1549–1626)

Scholars know the story of one slave of this period because of his success as a military commander in India. When converted to Islam, he was re-named Malik Amber, and that is how history knows him. He was born in 1548 in the city of Harar on the Ethiopian high plateau and, according to one manuscript, sold into slavery by his parents around 1565. Malik Amber walked, probably chained, the four hundred miles from Harar on the Ethiopian plain north to Massawa (current-day Mits'iwa), a set of small islands just off the western coast of the Red Sea that provided shelter against storms. The islands formed the only port along five hundred miles of coastline. The Portuguese, at about the time Malik Amber passed through, found that the islands had forty-nine

---

16. Francisco Alvarez, *Narrative of the Portuguese Embassy to Abyssinia during the Years 1520–1527*, trans. Lord Stanley of Alderley (London: Hakluyt Society, 1881), 111–12.

A nineteenth-century etching of the Devagiri Fortress (also known as Daulatabad), which was taken by Malik Amber's African slave army around the time of his usurpation of the throne in 1607.

large cisterns that stored rainwater, but all the island's food supply came from the mainland. Cows were inexpensive. According to one source, "however big it [a cow] may be, [it] is not worth more than four or five pieces of linen."[17] The population of Massawa was perhaps three thousand; observers noted that the population doubled with the arrival of a big slave caravan.

The next stop after Massawa for slaves on the route to Baghdad was a large port, such as Mocha or Aden, near the mouth of the Red Sea. A Dutch memoir from the period recounts that Malik Amber was sold in Mocha for twenty ducats.[18] We do not know if he was taken up the Red Sea to Jiddah and overland to Baghdad or via Kish, the Persian Gulf, and up the Euphrates River. Regardless of his itinerary, Malik Amber was

17. See Anthony d'Avray, *Lords of the Red Sea: The History of a Red Sea Society from the Sixteenth to the Nineteenth Centuries* (Wiesbaden, Germany: Harrassowitz, 1966), 73–74.

18. The Venetian ducat, each 3.545 grams of pure gold, had become a global coin in the sixteenth century because of its purity and high value. By way of comparison, around 1565, the retail price in Italy for a printed book, a rather costly item, averaged around three and a half ducats.

sold in Baghdad to a merchant who trained him in Persian and in the skills of a soldier. A few years later the merchant took him via the Persian Gulf and the Indian Ocean to northwestern India and sold him in a group of one thousand African male slaves. The buyer was a high noble of the Ahmednagar Sultanate (1490–1636), himself an ex-slave traded from Ethiopia.

Malik Amber began his military career as a simple soldier in the service of the noble who purchased him. Through factional feuds, invasions, and raiding warfare, he showed his military prowess and became a leader of men. His commands increased from a few hundred to a thousand, eventually to more

Malik Amber would have dressed much like this portrait of another elite African in seventeenth-century India whose name is unknown. Museum of Islamic Art, Doha.

than ten thousand slave soldiers. He became adept at internal and external politics, gained his freedom, fought off larger invading forces, seized the throne of Ahmadnagar, and at his death, passed it on to his son.

The phase of African slave armies in southern India was, however, not to last. By about 1650 a new group of free local Indian cavalry, the Marathas, supplanted the African slave soldiers. They were far less expensive because they went back to their farms during the period of monsoon rains, and they were more mobile, riding small local horses. These Marathas came to dominate war and politics in southern India for more than a century.

East African Slavery: 1300 to 1600

The earliest firm evidence of the expansion of slaving farther south along the coast of East Africa comes from Ibn Battuta, the famous fourteenth-century Muslim traveler. He arrived at Kilwa, a prosperous port on the coast of current-day Tanzania, and observed that the Islamic king "used to engage frequently in expeditions to the land of the Zinj people [inland peoples], raiding them and taking booty." Ibn Battuta further observed the king gives ten slaves to a man he wants to honor.[19]

New ports developed, not just at Kilwa, but at Mombasa, the Pemba Islands, and Zanzibar. In these new ports many local traders converted to Islam, bought Indian cloth, changed their dress to look like the seafaring Arabs with whom they traded, and defined themselves as *Swahili*, that is, people of the coast (*sahil* in Arabic), as opposed to inland people. These successful local slave traders built large stone houses and kept slaves for domestic and farm work. They also developed fictionalized genealogies that traced descent from Arab or Iranian traders and changed their culture to emphasize urbanity and gentility. A polyglot language, known as Kiswahili, developed from the local Bantu language with an admixture of Arabic and became the language of trade even in areas far inland from the coast. Coastal port cities were often at war with each other over the trade in gold from the Zambezi River area, ivory and slaves from the interior.[20]

The Final Phase of the East African Slave Trade

The last phase of the East African slave trade (1600–1920) featured foreign intervention along the coast. It began in the 1500s with the Portuguese defeating the Ottoman Empire for naval control of the Indian Ocean and seizing ports: Goa, Aden, Mombasa, Muscat, the island of Socotra off the Horn of Africa, and the island of Mozambique. From

---

19. *The Travels of Ibn Battuta, A.D. 1325–1354*, trans. H. A. R. Gibb (New Delhi, India: Munshiram Manoharlal, 1993), 2:380–81.

20. The peoples of the interior were by no means all small groups. In the present country of Zimbabwe are the ruins of Great Zimbabwe, the capital of a large kingdom that existed from ca. 1100 to ca. 1450. It might have had a population of eighteen thousand. Gold mines in the area were the basis of its wealth. In addition to this presumed capital city, there exist ruins of several hundred small towns of the same period and architectural style.

these fortified outposts the Portuguese cruised the sea-lanes and tried to control and tax all trade on the Indian Ocean. At best, the Portuguese were only partially successful. Local shipyards built faster vessels, capable of outrunning Portuguese patrols. Within a century the grand Portuguese design had failed. It proved too costly to try to patrol and tax an entire ocean.

The Portuguese effort, however, had three important effects on East African slavery. First, it connected the Atlantic Ocean with the Indian Ocean. This meant that when the demand for slaves in the Americas sharply increased in the eighteenth century, the East African coast became a source of slaves. Second, the Portuguese left small enclaves on the East Coast, which later served as slaving stations when the rest of the European countries had made slaving illegal. Third, the Portuguese conquest of Oman (a sultanate on the southeast coast of the Arabian Peninsula, bordering the Indian Ocean) not only produced a counterattack by the Omanis, which cleared the mainland, but also triggered a naval war for control of the western Indian Ocean. In 1698 the Omanis captured Zanzibar Island and established themselves as the principal slavers of East Africa. At first their expanded trade followed the usual monsoon pattern to the Middle East and had strong ties between the ruling house of Oman and the provincial governors in Zanzibar.

In the eighteenth and nineteenth centuries, Omani slavers based in Zanzibar connected with the new demand for slaves by European colonies. In the 1700s, on two uninhabited islands (Isle de France and Isle Bourbon) about five hundred miles off the East African coast, the French developed sugar plantations on the model of similar plantations in the Caribbean. Zanzibar sold thousands of captured slaves to clear the land and work these plantations. The sultan of Zanzibar developed his own clove plantations on the forested hills of the island along the same model. Slaves were also regularly shipped around the Cape of Good Hope to the plantations of the Americas. In the nineteenth century, more than a million slaves were captured and shipped from East Africa.

All of this began to shift with the anti-slavery movement in Great Britain in the early decades of the nineteenth century. By 1833, slavery was illegal in all British territories. This legislation had little effect except in a few specific places in East Africa. England, however, took control of Mauritius after the defeat of Napoleon and developed it as a naval base. England well recognized that much of the East African slave trading went through Portuguese ports and territory. An Anglo-Portuguese Treaty of 1842 stipulated that, among many other provisions, English ships could seize slave-trading ships in the Indian Ocean, even if the evidence was only shackles or chains.

By the late nineteenth century on the East African coast, faster British steam vessels routinely intercepted slower slave ships under sail. The British were also powerful enough in the Mediterranean to put pressure on the long-standing sources of demand for slaves, especially Egypt and the Ottoman Empire. British embassies and ships in the Mediterranean often welcomed runaway slaves and tried to find employment for them.

In spite of British attempts at interdiction, the East African slave trade lasted well into the twentieth century. World War I (1914–1918) ended the Ottoman Empire, and the modernizing impetus under the leader of Turkish independence, Mustafa Kemal Ataturk, promulgated a new civil code and criminal code, which made slavery and the slave trade illegal. Perhaps the last large-scale movement of East African slaves to the Middle East was in the 1920s. A boom in date production, based on the new popularity of dates as a Christmas delicacy in the United States, resulted in new date plantations. Imported African slaves opened the land and worked the plantations. The boom in date production collapsed in the Depression of the 1930s.

Conclusions

What, then, were the numbers of people reduced to slavery and brought from the East African interior to the port cities of the coast, Ethiopia, Egypt, the Middle East, and India, over the 1,500-year history of the route? Admittedly, there are no censuses of slaves. Even runs of tax data that include slaves are only found for the nineteenth century. Nevertheless, though not considered particularly reliable, some documents record statistics on African slaves, such as the seven thousand African slaves in the caliph's palace alone in the 800s and 900s. Some portion of the estimated one-hundred-thousand-man army of the Zanj Rebellion were East African slaves. Documents also suggest a ten-thousand-man African slave army in western India in the 1600s. Considerably more reliable are British records of their interceptions of slave ships in the nineteenth century. Some years ago Patrick Manning, historian of the African diaspora, estimated that seven million slaves were shipped along this route between about 1500 and the end of the slave trade in the twentieth century.[21] To get to some sort of numeric total, we need to add the slaves transported before 1500, such as slaves from Nubia transported down the Nile through much of the three-thousand-year-long dynastic history of Egypt. An additional million might plausibly cover the period before 1500 CE, bringing the total of slaves transported from East Africa to about eight million. Both ships and infrastructure were quite adequate to deal with these sorts of numbers.

And what were the long-term effects of the East African slave trade? First and foremost was the human cost of the men, women, and children who were brutalized and branded or killed or allowed to die in the process of capture and transportation. Those who survived were uprooted from their homes and families and sent to serve without prospects in places where they had to change their name, religion, and culture. Slavery destroyed communities and depopulated whole areas. No amount of individual success by a few military slaves, such as Malik Amber, can weigh against this overall suffering and dislocation. In East Africa (very much as was also the case in West and North Africa), slavery defined a predatory relationship between the coast and the interior from Ethiopia south all the way to Zanzibar. Hostility, distrust, and suspicion between peoples of the interior and the coast are still characteristic of countries along the East African coast. Where there was a long tradition of war and slaving, intertribal hostility remains strong.

It is perhaps worth reiterating that over the long history of trade in the Indian Ocean, much more than slaves traveled between the Middle East, Africa, and India. To Africa from India came the banana, rice, tea, and many Indian words. Tropical medicines from India were a routine part of the Swahili pharmacopoeia. Islam moved south from the Middle East to Africa and east to India. From the early centuries CE, western India supplied the East African demand for cotton cloth. Traders brought back requests, and workshops supplied special patterns and colors, even specific patterns for specific tribes.

And what of slavery today in both East Africa and the regions that were the long-standing sources of demand for slaves? The Arab-style

---

21. Patrick Manning, *Slavery and African Life: Occidental, Oriental, and African Slave Trades* (Cambridge: Cambridge University Press: 1990), chap. 4.

sailing vessels known as dhows, which were the backbone of the East African slave trade, are gone. The last voyages from the west coast of India to Africa ended in the 1970s. All of the former slave-supplying regions are now independent countries, such as Kenya and Tanzania, and have laws against slavery. Similar laws now exist in the demand areas, for example, Turkey, Iraq, and Egypt. These laws, however, do not mean that slavery has ended, but the practice is very different from older slaving on the East African coast. Slavery now tends to be the result of serious economic inequality or war. In Egypt, for example, there are still reports of daughters of poor families sold into domestic service with rich families. Reports circulate of enslavement by Arab raiders in the warfare in Sudan. The larger world, unlike the period of the East African slave trade, sees these enslavements as wrong, unnatural, and immoral. We will further explore these issues in Chapter 4.

Sources

Early Slave Trading on the East African Coast: A Tall Tale

Buzurg ibn Shahriyar, who lived in the first half of the tenth century, was a Persian captain of a merchant ship. At the port of Siraf in the Persian Gulf in the middle of the tenth century, he wrote down stories he heard from other sailors. Our selection is a plausibly entertaining story that he recorded, suggestive of some features of an early East African slave trade. Note that the Arabs claim to have been blown off course to Sofala, an ancient port about two hundred miles south of the mouth of the Zambezi River in present-day Mozambique. This port is over a thousand miles south of the normal monsoon routes to the Zanzibar region of present-day Tanzania. Note the similarities to the story of Malik Amber: transportation to a port serving the inland Middle East; sale to a relatively kind owner in Baghdad; and conversion to Islam. In the last portion of the story, note how the king has a certain fellow feeling toward the sailors because they are all Muslims, even though he knows the sailors are scoundrels.

A Question for Consideration

This tall tale apparently contains a substratum of truth. Which elements of it reflect features and consequences of the East African slave trade? Be as specific as possible.

✦✦✦✦✦

Buzurg ibn Shahriyar, *Book of the Wonders of India*[22]

Ismailawaih told me and several sailors who were with him, that he departed Oman in his ship to go to Kabila[23] in the year 310 [922 CE].[24] A storm drove him toward Sofala in the land of the Zanj. Seeing the coast where we were . . . and recognizing that we were falling among black eaters of human flesh[25] and certain to perish, we made our ablutions[26] and turned our hearts to God, reciting for one another the prayer for the dead. The canoes of the Negroes encircled us and brought us into the harbor. We cast anchor and went ashore. They conducted us to their king. He was a young Negro, handsome and well built. He asked us who we were and where we were headed. We replied that the goal of our voyage was his very country.

"You lie," he said. "It is not our homeland where you planned to disembark. It is only the winds that have driven you, despite

22. Buzurg ibn Shahriyar, *Les merveilles de l'Inde: ourage arabe inédite du Xe siècle*, trans. L. Marcel Devic (Paris: A. Lemerre, 1878), 43–52, passim (translated into English by A. J. Andrea; all rights reserved).
23. Both a Hindi and a Swahili word that means "tribe" or "clan." It probably refers to his intention to sail either to the Swahili Coast or (less likely) the western coast of India.
24. The year AH 310 (Anno Hegirae, "In the year of the Hijra"). The Islamic calendar is calculated from the Prophet's *hijra*, or journey, from Mecca to Medina in 622 CE. Because the Islamic calendar is lunar, consisting of 354 days, one cannot simply add 622 to any Muslim year to arrive at its Gregorian, or CE, counterpart.
25. Some peoples of the Congo Basin that lies farther to the west were rumored to practice cannibalism, but it is equally unlikely that any people of the East Coast did so.
26. Prior to prayer, Muslims ritually wash portions of their bodies.

yourselves, onto our shores." When we confessed that he spoke the truth, he said: "Unload your merchandise. Sell and buy. You have nothing to fear."

We placed our bundles of goods on shore and began to trade, an excellent trade for us that was without any obstacle or customs dues. We gave him a few presents to which he reciprocated with gifts of equal worth or yet ones of even greater value. . . . Our stay there lasted several months. When the time to depart came, we asked his permission to go, which he granted us immediately. They loaded the goods that we had purchased and business was concluded. With everything in order, the king was aware of our intention to again set sail. He accompanied us to the shore with some of his people, got into one of the boats, and came out to the ship with us. He even came on board with seven of his companions.

When I saw them there, I said to myself: "This young king would certainly sell for the high price of thirty dinars in the Oman market, and sixty dinars for his seven companions. . . . Their clothes are not worth less than twenty dinars. Altogether, this would give us a profit of at least 3,000 dirhams,[27] without any trouble." Reflecting thus, I gave the crew their orders. They set the sails and weighed anchor.

Meanwhile, the king gave us a thousand friendly good-byes, engaging us to return again and promising us a warm welcome upon our return. When he saw the sails fill with wind and the ship begin its voyage, his face changed. "You are underway," he said. "Ah, well. I must say farewell to you." And he wished to climb down into their canoes, which were moored along side [the ship]. But we cut the ropes and said to him: "You will stay with us; we will take you to our country. There we will reward you for all of your kindnesses to us."

"Strangers," he said, "when you fell onto our beaches, my people wished to eat you and pillage your goods, as they have already done to others like you. But I have protected you, asking

---

27. By Islamic law, a dinar was a coin of pure gold, weighing 4.25 grams. A dirham was a coin of pure silver weighing 2.975 grams. Traditionally, seven dinars weighed the equivalent of ten dirhams. Ismailawaih's calculation of 110 dinars being worth 3,000 dirhams was based on the relative value of gold to silver, not on the weight of the coins.

nothing from you. As a token of my goodwill, I came down to bid you farewell on your own ship. Treat me then as justice demands, and let me go on my own way to my country."

But no one paid any attention to his words. No notice was taken of them. And as the wind got up, the coast was not slow in disappearing from our eyes. Then night enveloped us in its veil, and we entered the open sea.

When day arrived, the king and his companions were put with the other slaves, whose number reached about two hundred heads. He was not treated differently from his companions in captivity. The king spoke not a word and did not even open his mouth. He behaved as if we were unknown to him and as if we did not know him. When we arrived at Oman, the slaves were sold, and the king with them.

Now, several years later, as we were sailing from Oman to Kabila, the wind drove us again toward the coasts of Sofala of the Zanj people, and we arrived at precisely the same place. The Negroes saw us, their canoes surrounded us, and we recognized one another. Fully certain that we would perish this time, terror struck us dumb. We performed ablutions in silence, recited the prayer of the dead, and said farewell to one another. The Negroes seized us, conducted us to the king's dwelling, and made us go in. Imagine our surprise; it was the same king that we had known, seated on his throne, as if we had left him there. We prostrated ourselves before him, overcome, and had not the strength to raise ourselves up.

"Ahah! Here are my old friends," he said. Not one of us was capable of a response. We trembled throughout our bodies. He continued: "Come, raise your heads. I grant you an *aman* for your persons and goods."[28] Some raised their heads; others lacked the strength, overcome with shame. But he showed himself gentle and gracious until we all raised our heads, but not daring to look him in the face, so much were we moved by remorse and fear. When, reassured by his *aman*, we finally recovered our senses, he said: "Ah! Traitors! How you treated me after what I did for you!" And each of us cried out: "Mercy, Your Majesty! Be

---

28. "Peace" or "security" in Arabic, an *aman* is a safe conduct pass.

merciful!" "I will be merciful," he said. "Go on as before with your business of buying and selling. You may trade with full liberty."

We could not believe our ears. We feared that this was nothing other than an act of treachery to induce us to unload our merchandise. Nevertheless, we brought the goods to shore, and we went to him, offering a gift of tremendous value. But he refused it, saying: "You are unworthy of my accepting a gift from you. I will not sully my property with anything that would come from you."

After that we conducted our business in peace. When it was time to depart, we requested permission to embark. He accommodated us. At the moment of departure, I went to give him the news. "Go," he said, "under the protection of God." "Your Majesty," I replied, "you have rained down your goodness upon us, and we have been ungrateful and traitorous toward you. But how did you escape and return to your country?"

[The king tells his story. Upon being sold in Oman, he was taken to Basra, where he was instructed in the practices and faith of Islam. He was subsequently re-sold and brought to Baghdad, where he learned Arabic and continued his conversion to Islam. Eventually he escaped in a pilgrim caravan to Mecca and performed the *hajj*. From Mecca, he traveled with a returning-pilgrim caravan to Cairo. From there he followed the Nile south, knowing that its source was in the land of the Zanj. In his travels he fell in among some disreputable Blacks who enslaved him. He escaped. He was again captured and enslaved and escaped once more. Finally, he reached the land of the Zanj. Eventually, he reached the sea and took a boat to the shores of his home country, where he learned that his people had agreed not to have another king until they were certain of his fate, for they had been told that he was still alive, healthy, and safe in the land of the Arabs. He then continues.]

"When the day came, I went into town and headed toward my palace. I found my family just as I had left it, but plunged into grief. My kinfolk listened to the account of my story, which surprised them and filled them with joy. They embraced, as did I, the religion of Islam. And so I returned to possession of my sovereignty—a month before you arrived. And, behold, here I am, happy and satisfied with the grace that God has given me and mine of knowing the precepts of Islam, the true faith, prayers, fasting, the pilgrimage, and what is permitted and what is forbidden. For no other person in the land of Zanj has obtained a similar favor. And if I have forgiven you it is because you were the first cause of the purity of my religion. But there rests on my conscience one matter. I pray God to take this sin away from me." "What is this thing, Your Majesty?" I asked. "It is," he said, "that when leaving Baghdad, I left my master without his permission, and I have not returned to him. If I were to meet an honest man, I would ask him to take the price of my purchase to my master. If there were among you a good man, if you were upright men, I would give you a sum of money to give him—a sum ten times what he paid as compensation for the delay. But you are nothing but traitors and swindlers."

We made our good-byes to him. "Go," he said, "and if you return to us, I shall not treat you differently from what I have done. You will receive the best welcome. And Muslims may know that they may come here to us, as to brothers, Muslims like themselves. As for accompanying you to your ship, I have reasons for not doing so." At that point we parted.

◆ ◆ ◆ ◆ ◆

The Istanbul Slave Market, 1843

This description of the Istanbul slave market in the 1840s is by Charles White, part of a British business and diplomatic community of perhaps three thousand men and women in Istanbul of the time. Istanbul (earlier Constantinople) had been a slave destination for more than 1,500 years and received slaves from the East African coast, Ethiopia, and the trans-Saharan slave trade, as well as from numerous other places in Eurasia.

A painting of the Istanbul Slave Market (Esir Pazari) by David Allan (1836). The Nur-i Osmaniye Mosque is in the background. An excellent example of Romantic Orientalism, this rendition of the slave market combines exoticism with eroticism—characteristics typical of this European genre. (CC-BY-SA 3.0 license.)

Questions for Consideration

What were the categories of slaves, and how did the architecture of the market reinforce these categories? What added to or decreased the sale price of a slave? Evidence from accounts by Western visitors to the slave market (which was a popular tourist attraction) leads historians to conclude that almost all slaves bought and sold in Istanbul's slave market were destined for domestic service. What is the evidence in this account that supports that conclusion? Is there any contrary evidence? Note the estimated death rates for slaves before they arrived in Istanbul. How believable is it? Support your answer. How far geographically was the draw of the Istanbul slave market, even in its waning years? What sorts of education and language training might it take to make a productive slave in this market?

✦✦✦✦✦

Charles White, *Three Years in Constantinople*[29]

According to tradition, the existing market owes its origin to the following circumstance. Mohammed II, being upon his way from the waterside to the At Maidany,[30] chanced to pass through this place, which was obstructed on all sides by slaves and dealers.[31] His horse, a fiery animal, alarmed at the clanking of the captives' chains, became restive, and, after striking furiously with its fore legs, slew a female Christian captive with a child in her arms. At this sight the Sultan was much moved, and therefore, in order to prevent the recurrence of such misfortunes, he directed that a regular market should be constructed, and placed under the superintendence of proper officers. The building was originally destined for the sale of captives, thence its name, which signifies a prisoner taken in war, rather than a menial slave (*keool*).

The aspect of Yessir Bazary[32] sorrowfully harmonizes with its destination and the degraded condition of its temporary inmates. It is entered by a large wooden gate, open during business hours, that is, from eight a.m. to mid-day, excepting upon Fridays, when it is closed to purchasers.[33] This gate is [staffed by a guard], whose duty it is to watch persons passing to and fro, and to give alarm, should slaves attempt to escape. But this is nearly impossible, as the chambers or cells are locked up

---

29. Charles White, *Three Years in Constantinople* (London: H. Colburn, 1845), 2:146–52.
30. The area of the Roman-Byzantine Hippodrome (Chariot-racing stadium), which today is the heart of Sultanahmet (the area around the so-called Blue Mosque). Descriptions and paintings of the slave market place it a bit less than a mile west of the Hippodrome and very near the Grand Bazaar, which every tourist visits today.
31. This incident, based on a piece of hearsay information and questionable as evidence, presumably refers to Sultan Mehmed II, who in 1453 conquered Constantinople (today Istanbul), the last remnant of the Christian Byzantine Empire.
32. The *Esir Pazari*, or slave market, which apparently was located on the site of the earlier Byzantine slave market. The market became known popularly as the Aurat (or Avret) Bazaar, which means the "Women's [slave] Market."
33. Friday is holy to Muslims, and no slaves would have been bought or sold on that day. By law, only Muslims could purchase slaves at this market, and all slaves had to be non-Muslims.

soon after mid-day, and the laws relating to the abstraction or harbouring of runaway slaves are peremptory.[34]

The interior consists of an irregular quadrangle. . . . In the centre is a detached building, the upper portion serving as lodgings for . . . slavedealers, and underneath are cells for . . . (slaves newly imported). To this is attached a coffee-house, and near to it is a half ruined mosque. Around the three habitable sides of the court runs an open colonnade, supported by wooden columns, and approached by steps at the angles. Under the colonnade are platforms, separated from each other by low railings and benches. Upon these, dealers and customers may be seen seated during business hours smoking and discussing prices.

Behind these platforms are ranges of small chambers, divided into two compartments by a trellice-work. The habitable part is raised about three feet from the ground; the remainder serves as passage and cooking-place. The front portion is generally tenanted by black, and the back by white, slaves. These chambers are exclusively devoted to females.[35] Those to the north and west are destined for second-hand negresses (Arab), or white women (*beiaz*)—that is, for slaves who have been previously purchased and instructed, and are sent to be resold, perhaps a second or third time. Some are known to have been resold many times. The hovels to the east are reserved for newly-imported negresses, or black and white women of low price.

The platforms are divided from the chambers by a narrow alley, on the wall side of which are benches, where black women are exposed for sale. This alley serves as a passage of communication and walk for the [brokers], who sell slaves by auction and on commission.[36] In this case, the brokers walk round, followed by the slaves, and announce the price offered. Purchasers, seated upon the platforms, then examine, question, and bid, as suits their fancy, until at length the woman is sold or withdrawn.

---

34. The sentence for harboring a runaway slave would have been death.

35. An eyewitness account of 1839 by Edmund Spencer informs us that the ground floor was for blacks, whereas the upper floor housed the more desirable "beauties" from Circassia, Georgia, and Greece.

36. Evidence shows that these slave brokers were of both sexes—women as well as men.

When weather permits, the newly imported black females are called forth, mats are spread in front of the central building, and they are seated unveiled in groups and lines to await purchasers. The dress of these poor creatures, mostly young girls from ten to fifteen years of age, consists of a red-striped cotton handkerchief twined round the head, a pair of coarse linen drawers, and the common Arab or Egyptian linen *abba* (wrapper), which serves as veil and robe. Some wear brass anklets and bracelets riveted on the leg or arm.

The chambers to the north and west are occupied by second-hand slaves. When black women are thus resold, their value often increases, because they have generally been instructed in domestic duties, especially in the culinary art, for which purpose they are employed in all families where male artists do not form a part of the household. But the value of white women generally decreases from twenty to forty per cent, as no one parts with a female of this colour unless from profligate motive or incorrigible defects. It is no uncommon practice with young and wealthy libertines to purchase young women from the Circassian dealers . . . or from those who buy women from the latter to educate and resell, and then, at the expiration of a few weeks, to send them to Yessir Bazary, in order to procure money for purchasing other novelties.

The principal and favourite marts for the supply of negresses are Tripoli and Tunis.[37] Regular dealers, almost all Arabs, trade between Stambol[38] and these places at stated periods. They purchase their human merchandize from the Arabs dealing with the interior, and ship them for the Bosphorus,[39] where about two thirds are disposed of in the city, and the remainder for the interior and Persia.

An old Arab, who, "with Allah's permission" had carried on the trade during many years, informed me that it was a profitable

---

37. Two cities of western North Africa. Negroid slaves were transported there via the overland caravan routes from sub-Saharan West Africa, where they had been exchanged for salt, manufactured goods, and horses.

38. Another way of saying "Istanbul." Istanbul is the Turkish variant on a Byzantine Greek nickname for Constantinople, *eis ten Polin*, which means "in the City."

39. The strait, or narrow body of water, that connects the Black Sea with the Sea of Marmara and flows past Constantinople/Istanbul.

business, and, as he cleared about thirty per cent by his bargains, he hoped to continue so to do until he quitted this perishable world for the gardens of Paradise. According to his statement, the profits of the original dealers and Stambol merchants would be enormous, were it not for the great mortality that invariably occurs among their unhappy merchandize, which, from the period of their quitting Fezzan,[40] or other places in the interior of Africa, until their arrival at Stambol, exceeds sixty per cent.

Notwithstanding this, the average price of strong newly imported slaves at Yessir Bazary is as low as 1,500 piastres . . . and never exceeds 2,500. The ordinary price for second-hand slaves, clean, healthy, and well instructed, averages from 2,500 to 3,000, and never exceeds 5,000. White women sold in this bazar, when young and without defects, average from 10 to 15,000 piastres.[41] The maximum, according to the dellal [dealer], was 45,000; but this is rare, and only in cases of great beauty, extraordinary accomplishments, and virginity, as sometimes occurs when death of proprietors, or other circumstances, throw the whole contents of a harem on the market.

Slaves brought from Egypt, that is, the blacks of Sennal and the higher regions,[42] are not in such request as those imported via Tripoli. They are regarded as belonging to the "race of Pharaoh," inapt to learn, stubborn, and neither diligent nor trustworthy.

◆◆◆◆◆

British Anti-Slaving Naval Patrols

In the 1840s the British navy began patrolling the East African coast to break up the slave trade. The trade was still quite legal on land but

---

40. The southwestern region of present-day Libya.

41. As a rough comparison, a skilled shipbuilder or a miner in England at the time made annually about three to four times the cost of a slave in Istanbul. Teachers made four to five times the cost of a slave.

42. The author presumably means Sudan and the upper reaches of the Nile.

illegal on the seas, as laid out in the treaty between England and Portugal signed in 1842, which is discussed above. This account was written by Lieutenant Frederick Barnard, who served on a British naval vessel that patrolled the channel between the Mozambique coast and the island of Madagascar, 1842–1845.

Questions for Consideration

What can we infer from this account about conditions aboard the ship for the slaves before its capture? There were more than two hundred slaves aboard the ship when it was captured. Knowing that, what do you conclude about the mortality rate for slaves in these conditions?

◆◆◆◆◆

Frederick Lamport Barnard, *Three Years' Cruize in the Mozambique Channel for the Suppression of the Slave Trade*[43]

A day or two afterwards . . . I accompanied Dr. Kittle on board [the captured slave ship] to pick out fifty of the most healthy boys to take to the ship, that the others might have more room, and the scene on board beggars all description. On the day she was captured the slaves broke open the casks of *aqua ardient* [alcohol] which some of them drank in large quantities: others took salt water, salt beef, and pork, and raw fowls, in consequence of which fifty died the first night, which unfortunately was squally; and to save the vessel the poor wretches were obliged to be kept below, or run the risk of being washed overboard. Previous to this, however, many of the dead bodies were seen on the slave-deck by our men who went down for water, and others were in such a state from their excesses, that in all probability the

---

43. Frederick Lamport Barnard, *Three Years' Cruize in the Mozambique Channel for the Suppression of the Slave Trade* (London: Richard Bentley, 1848).

mortality would have been nearly as great, even had they not been kept below. . . .

****

The slave-deck measured forty-six feet long twenty-five feet wide, and three feet, six inches high. Of the fifty that we took on board, forty nine arrived safely at the Cape, one having fallen into a tub during the night, and being too weak to crawl out, was smothered. We managed to clothe them all, cutting up table-covers, old green baize, and each contributing something. They were numbered and divided into two gangs, and a captain chosen from among them for each gang. They were made to run around the decks, for they were so pinched with cold, that had it not been for exercise, they would have doubled up like bootjacks and died.

◆◆◆◆◆

Slave Raids and Slave Liberation Near the Zambezi River

David Livingstone was the most famous English explorer of East Africa in the mid-nineteenth century. He was also an ardent opponent of slavery and the slave trade. In 1858 he returned to East Africa to explore the Zambezi River, which runs through current-day Mozambique. The intent of the expedition was to establish friendly relations with local chiefs, survey a promising site for a Christian mission, and expose and disrupt the slave trade. This excerpt from his journal finds the expedition more than three hundred miles up the Zambezi River. What particularly irritated Livingstone was that slavers were following his expedition, attacking all those who were befriended by the whites. Livingstone discovered that all the captured slaves were bound for the Portuguese town of Tette, about 150 miles inland on the Zambezi River.

Questions for Consideration

What were the conditions under which these slaves were marched? What can we infer about the "black drivers" of these slaves? Do you find anything surprising in your answer?

GANG OF CAPTIVES MET AT MBAME'S ON THEIR WAY TO TETTE.

David Livingstone, the famous African explorer, freed this line of captured slaves in 1845. Courtesy of the AGH Archives, Milwaukee.

✦✦✦✦✦

David Livingstone, *Narrative of an Expedition to the Zambesi*[44]

[A] long line of manacled men, women, and children, came wending their way round the hill and into the valley, on the side of which the village stood. The black drivers, armed with muskets, and bedecked with various articles of finery, marched jauntily in the front, middle, and rear of the line; some of them blowing exultant notes out of long tin horns. They seemed to feel that they were doing a very noble thing, and might proudly march with an air of triumph; but the instant the fellows caught a glimpse of the English, they darted off like mad into the forest—so fast, indeed, that we caught but a glimpse of their red caps and the soles of their feet. The chief of the party alone

44. David Livingstone, *Narrative of an Expedition to the Zambesi and Its Tributaries; and of the Discovery of the Lakes Shirwa and Nyassa, 1858–1864* (New York: Harper & Bros., 1866), 377.

remained; and he ... proved to be a well known slave of the late Commandant at Tette, and for some time our own attendant while there.

On asking him how he obtained these captives, he replied, he had bought them; but on our inquiring of the people themselves, all, save four, said they had been captured in war. While this inquiry was going on, he bolted too.

The captives knelt down, and, in their way of expressing thanks, clapped their hands with great energy. They were thus left entirely on our hands, and knives were soon busy at work cutting the women and children loose. It was more difficult to cut the men adrift, as each had his neck in the fork of a stout stick, six or seven feet long, and kept in by an iron rod which was riveted at both ends across the throat. With a saw, luckily in the bishop's baggage, one by one the men were sawn out into freedom. The women, on being told to take the meal they were carrying and cook breakfast for themselves and the children, seemed to consider the news too good to be true; but, after a little coaxing, went at it with alacrity, and made a capital fire by which to boil their pots with the slave sticks and bonds, their old acquaintances through many a sad night and weary day. Many were mere children about five years of age and under. One little boy, with the simplicity of childhood, said to our men, "The others tied and starved us; you cut the ropes and tell us to eat; what sort of people are you? Where did you come from?"

Two of the women had been shot the day before for attempting to untie the thongs. This, the rest were told, was to prevent them from attempting to escape. One woman had her infant's brains knocked out because she could not carry her load and it; and a man was dispatched with an axe because he had broken down with fatigue. Self-interest would have set a watch over the whole rather than commit murder; but in this traffic we invariably find self-interest overcome by contempt of human life and by blood-thirstiness.

Chapter 3

Slavery along the Barbary Coast

Slavery based on the Barbary Coast of North Africa (today Algeria, Tunisia, and Morocco) from about 1500 to the late 1700s was a vast and profitable enterprise.[1] Five central features confound our image of slavery, which is based on slavery in the Americas. First is the issue of race. Instead of African blacks, Mediterranean slaves were largely whites from Western Europe, which contained some of the most powerful nations on earth at the time. The slaveholders were not whites but darker-skinned North Africans and Middle Easterners. Second, religion rather than race underlay the politics and economics of Mediterranean slave taking. Muslim slavers captured Christian slaves as part of recurrent warfare between Christian powers north of the Mediterranean and Muslim powers south and east of the Mediterranean. Third, unlike slaves brought to the Americas, captured Europeans were not cut off from their families. Slaves were, in fact, encouraged to write home and tell their families of their plight because slaveholders hoped to extract ransom. Fourth, unlike the plight of African slaves in the New World, some European kingdoms, especially Spain and France, tried to locate and free their enslaved subjects. Along with the Catholic Church, they established consuls and legations in the capitals of the slaving kingdoms and tried to keep track of slaves. Finally, for historians researching this slaving world, a host of documents remain, such as letters dictated by illiterate slaves to literate slaves and sent to their families as well as to kings and the Church; lists of slaves and more

---

1. The origin of the term "Barbary" reflects the complexities of who was considered "civilized" and who was not in the Mediterranean world. The term is derived most directly from the term Berber, which now refers to peoples who share the Berber language group and are spread across a broad swath of western Africa that includes Morocco, southern Algeria, Mali, and Niger. Berber, however, is not an indigenous term for these language-related peoples. It was given to some northern branches of this language group by Romans who fought them in the first centuries CE. Their use of the term Berber (barbarian) had the same meaning throughout the Roman Empire: an uncivilized people who did not speak Latin. The term is, however, even older. The Romans borrowed the term from the Greek *barbaros*, meaning a non-Greek.

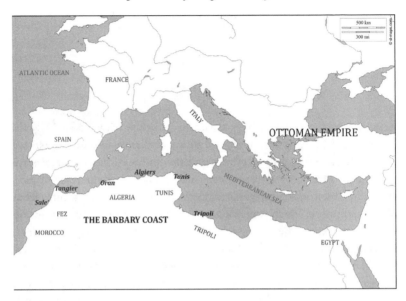

general reports by consuls and the Church; and narratives of those who escaped or were ransomed.

Slave's Work: Sea and Land

At the core of this Mediterranean slavery was the rowed galley, a seafaring technology particularly suited to the variable winds of the Mediterranean and well known to the ancient Phoenicians and Greeks. According to Homer, this type of ship carried Odysseus on his adventures returning from the Trojan Wars. Until the late seventeenth century the rowed galley remained the best technology for trade and warfare on the Mediterranean. From the time of the Phoenicians and Greeks onward, rowing a galley was extremely hard, dangerous, and brutal work. As we saw in Chapter 1, occasionally free men performed this work, such as citizens in the service of the city-state of Athens. Generally, however, rowing galleys was work that no free man would do. Slaves powered both ships of war and ships of trade.

Demand for galley slaves depended on the scope of trade as well as warfare in the Mediterranean. In times of relative peace the demand for galley slaves on trading ships rose. In times of war, especially when many powers were competing for control of portions of the Mediterranean, demand for slaves to row war galleys increased.

Surrounding this core of galley slavery were several other long-standing forms of slavery in the Mediterranean. Just as in Greek times, slaves, especially in the Middle East and North Africa, continued to do hard, dangerous work in mines, forests, and quarries. Slaves did much of the construction work in this region. (The tradition of slaves in construction work reaches back at least as far as biblical times, as described in the Book of Exodus.) Skilled slaves produced goods and services whose benefit went to their masters. Female slaves became concubines of their masters or performed the domestic drudgework of carrying water, cleaning the house, food preparation, and laundry. Some male slaves avoided the galleys and instead served in private households, cleaning the stables and serving as messengers, guards, and entertainers.

From about 1500 until the Battle of Lepanto in 1571 intermittent war for control of the Mediterranean Sea raged between the Muslim Ottoman Empire based in Istanbul, controlling the eastern Mediterranean, and various Catholic powers including Sicily, Venice, and the Hapsburg monarchy, which sent fleets from Spain.[2] Battles, both on land and sea, produced tens of thousands of slaves as war captives. In the same sixteenth century the Ottoman Empire slowly lost control of Algeria and Tunis, provinces on the North African coast. Slave capture, sale, and ransom formed the economic basis of these highly successful breakaways. Their coast, the Barbary, gave its name to slave-taking ships and their captains who wreaked havoc with Mediterranean shipping. Their shore raids on villages and towns produced terror along coastlines from Italy to Ireland. In 1544, for example, a Barbary slaver named Heyreddin enslaved nine thousand people, thereby virtually depopulating the island of Lipari, located just north of the eastern end of Sicily.

No modern scholar has yet attempted an overall census of slaves around the Mediterranean. Nevertheless, piecemeal studies of particular kingdoms and periods suggest that the scale of slavery was enormous. On the Barbary Coast, Algeria had the largest number of warships, at least sixty and possibly ninety at its peak strength. Tripoli had perhaps twenty-five; Tunis, fifteen to twenty; and Salé (along the Atlantic coast of Morocco),

---

2. There were other Catholic powers, such as the Hospitalers on Rhodes and later Malta, who fought the Ottomans as pirates. Pope Pius V's Holy League that fought at the Battle of Lepanto included, beyond the Hapsburg states of the empire and Spain-Sicily, such powers as Venice, Genoa, Savoy, Urbino, the Papal States, and the Hospitalers.

twenty-five to thirty.[3] A conservative estimate of the number of galley slaves needed by the combined Barbary States at any one time would be twenty-five to thirty-five thousand rowers. The actual number could be much higher. To the east, eighty thousand men were necessary merely to row the galleys of the Ottoman ruler. Throughout the sixteenth century, the numbers of galley slaves of the Christian opponents of the Ottoman Empire were similar, though the number declined in the seventeenth century as the European powers developed more sophisticated sailing vessels to replace galleys. To the Ottoman galley slaves must be added the surely larger number of domestic slaves in the cities of the Mediterranean world, such as Istanbul, Alexandria, Cairo, and Genoa.[4]

One scholar has estimated that through the sixteenth and seventeenth centuries, there were twenty-five thousand European slaves at all times in Algiers alone and another ten thousand in other cities along the North African coast.[5] These male slaves were not permitted to marry local women and, thus, produced no children. Therefore, every slave who died or became too weak to work had to be replaced. Perhaps 15 percent of slaves died every year. The tough ones survived bubonic plague and other deadly diseases, which were endemic along the North African coast. Significant numbers of Christian slaves converted to Islam and, thereby, escaped the galleys. Some were freed by their masters. A few slaves escaped, and some were ransomed. Overall, on the Barbary coast, perhaps one salve in four had to be replaced every year. These figures suggest that at least a million and perhaps a million and half European men passed through the Barbary slave prisons between 1530 and 1780.[6]

Perhaps the most surprising comparison is with the smaller scale of West African slave trade across the Atlantic to the Americas. From 1500 to 1700, Barbary slavery of white Europeans was—without adding the

---

3. Stephen Clissold, *The Barbary Slaves* (London: P. Elek, 1977), 34.

4. Regular trade had for centuries brought slaves across the brutally hot and dry eight-hundred- to one-thousand-mile-wide Sahara to Barbary. This trade continued during the period that Barbary ships seized and enslaved European men. The number of enslaved sub-Saharan African blacks was, however, much smaller than enslaved white Europeans. Many blacks became overseers of Europeans.

5. Robert C. Davis, *Christian Slaves, Muslim Masters: White Slavery in the Mediterranean, the Barbary Coast, and Italy, 1500–1800* (New York: Palgrave Macmillan, 2003), 13.

6. Ibid., 23.

more numerous slaves of the Eastern Mediterranean or even the number of West African black slaves transported across the Sahara—numerically larger than slaves captured and shipped from West Africa to the Atlantic world. In fact a single slaver from Tripoli or Algiers often seized more slaves in a single raiding season than the average of 3,200 slaves moved from West Africa to the Americas in a typical year.[7] This comparison would reverse in the eighteenth and nineteenth centuries, with the number of slaves shipped to the Americas spiking and the number going to Barbary sharply falling. Overall, the total number of slaves transported to the Americas was much higher than those transported to Barbary.

This mass of white European slaves came from Barbary slavers' attacks on merchant shipping and coastal raids. One contemporary source estimated that Algerians alone captured more than six hundred European ships just between 1605 and 1664. Barbary ships captured prizes far into the North Atlantic Ocean. Coastal raids included Italy, France, and Spain and reached as far north as the coasts of the Netherlands, England, Ireland, and Iceland. The vast majority of slaves taken, however, were from the coasts and waters of the Mediterranean Sea and the Atlantic Ocean immediately west of the Straits of Gibraltar.

One of the more interesting of the Barbary pirate port cities was Salé, which was located on Morocco's Atlantic coast (and today lies directly across a river from Rabat, the capital of the Kingdom of Morocco). Salé started slaving in the 1620s, considerably later than the other Barbary states, and ended as an independent pirate port with its capture by the king of Morocco in the 1640s. Its pirates, known as the Salé Rovers, continued their work under the protection of the Moroccan king and included several European captains. The Salé Rovers, using sailing ships, rather than galleys, attacked shipping in the North and South Atlantic and the Caribbean. Ships from Salé remained relatively small to clear the sand bar across its harbor.

Barbary Slave Capture

A typical Barbary slaving run included both attacks on coastal towns and on trading ships. Towns yielded less booty than merchant ships but

---

7. Patrick Manning, *The African Diaspora: A History through Culture* (New York: Columbia University Press, 2009), 23.

substantially more people. The raiders swept onto a beach, attacked the local church and disabled the bells so no alarm could be sounded, and rounded up locals before they could flee into the countryside. Slavers desecrated churches, burned crops, and slaughtered cattle to enhance the terror. They seized food and supplies. Farmers and fishermen were then herded into the jammed hold with crewmen and passengers of captured ships. In a particularly ironic twist, slavers returned to the ravaged village a few days later and offered, on the spot, a cut-rate ransom of captured villagers to avoid the trouble of sailing the slaves back to market.[8] Few poor families had the means to pay even this cut-rate price.

Capture at sea began with a merchantman, large or small, sighting a ship that changed course to intercept it. The merchant ship was generally slower and less heavily armed than the galleys of the Barbary slavers. Slavers employed common, yet deceptive pirate tactics to approach the merchant ship. The slaver flew expedient colors. In some decades treaties made the Barbary fleet allies of the English against Spain. The slaver might appear to approach the merchant ship as an apparent ally. At other times treaties might give the Barbary fleet the right to board ships in search of contraband goods belonging to an enemy, such as France or Spain. When these tactics failed, the slaver galley simply ran down the merchantman and stormed the ship. When it became clear that the merchant ship could not outrun the Barbary galley, panic ensued. Wealthy passengers frantically removed their fine clothes and sought simple peasant clothes, hoping that their ransom would be lower if the slavers did not know their true status. Just as frantically they tried to sew some money or jewels into the humble clothes to buy necessities in prison.

Once the slavers boarded and controlled the merchant ship, beating and humiliation began. Random physical violence induced terror, hopelessness, and finally passivity—all necessary to control the passengers and crew. Slavers identified wealthy passengers by their soft hands or beat a crewmember into identifying them. Priests were particularly valuable since slavers knew that the Catholic Church would ransom them. Slavers stripped those captured, seeking circumcised Jews, who, the slavers knew, would be ransomed by their family, their trading network, or their synagogue. The slavers beat passengers until they disclosed hidden riches. The captain and each member of the crew of the slave ship, even the slaves

---

8. Davis, *Christian Slaves*, 43.

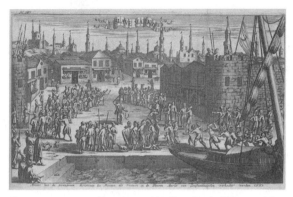

Slaves at auction in Algiers, ca. 1650. Rare Books Division, New York Public Library, Astor, Lenox, and Tilden Foundations.

rowing the galley, owned shares of everything seized.[9] Crew and passengers were chained together, locked into the hold, and kept for days without food or water. Eventually the imprisoned passengers and crew had to be fed. It was in everyone's interest that the new slaves remain in good enough shape to sell well in the slave market of Algiers or in other North African cities.

European Barbary Slavers

It is important to remember that, through the 1630s, the basic process of seizing ships and enslaving crews differed little whether the slavers were from Muslim Algiers or Christian cities north of the Mediterranean, such as Livorno, Naples, or Malta. Captured Muslims, Christians condemned by the Inquisition, and captured Protestants rowed galleys belonging to Christian cities. The larger political situation in Europe, however, produced allies for the Barbary slavers. In the first decades of the seventeenth century, the time of the Thirty Years War (1618–1648), France encouraged the Barbary slavers in attacks against rival Spain.

---

9. The share of loot assigned to the slaves rowing the galley was, of course, tiny. Even that portion was mainly claimed by the owners of the slaves. The assignment of shares of booty was common across the world at the time. The same system prevailed among pirates in the Caribbean and in the armies of the Mughals in their conquest of North India in the early sixteenth century.

Later in the seventeenth century, England encouraged Barbary ships to attack France and French ships.

A few Dutch and English corsairs used the Barbary as homeports for their raids on Spanish shipping. The most famous of these was John Ward (ca. 1553–1622), who, as a young sailor, served on ships that attacked Spanish vessels shipping. When peace between England and Spain eliminated Spanish vessels as targets, Ward and a group of sailors deserted the British navy, stole and captured successively larger warships, and sailed to the Mediterranean. He struck a deal with the ruler of Tunisia and used Tunis as his homeport. Though he attempted to return to England, the Crown would not pardon him. He lived in Tunis, converted to Islam, married an Italian woman, and remained a pirate and slaver until his death. Ward is credited with introducing square-rigged ships to the Barbary slavers and, thereby, prolonging their competitiveness with warships of other nations.

Slave Sale in Barbary

At the end of the slaving run, the galley returned to its homeport, firing guns and flying flags if it brought rich prizes. The bey claimed one-eighth of both the booty and the slaves, in addition to hulls of captured ships once they had been stripped. After the galley landed, the prisoners were paraded through the streets to general derision. They were called "Christian dogs," and small boys threw refuse at them. The procession ended at an overcrowded prison known as a *bagnio*. Each prisoner had his head and beard shaved and was fitted with an iron ring on his ankle, signifying slave status.

After the bey selected and removed his share of the slaves, the rest were sold, usually in the clothes in which they were captured, in a public market. An auctioneer lauded the virtues of each slave: how broad his back, how strong his arms, his skills, or how much he might bring in ransom. Buyers examined the teeth of slaves and had them stripped to reveal infirmities. Both the bey's agents and private buyers invested in slaves for labor, for skills they might have or, if they were perceived to be somewhat above common sailors or peasants, for their potential ransom. Buyers knew which countries were more likely to ransom their people. Working slaves went straight to the galleys, the mines, agriculture, or building sites. Skilled slaves went to workshops or the shipyards. Slaves bought by private owners carried water, washed walls, plastered and painted the house, did laundry, and took care of children. A few slaves, especially if they were literate, became overseers, accountants, or entertainers. Slaves bought for ransom moved into relative safety in private houses. The few enslaved women were converted to Islam and became concubines or entered domestic drudgery.

Slave Life on Sea and Land

Life on the galleys was almost unimaginably brutal and violent. Three to five men rowed each of the long sweeps. The galleys depended on speed, both to overtake merchant ships and to escape pursuit. At the slightest sign of slacking, an overseer lashed the bare back of the rower with a knotted rope. Day and night, rowers were chained to their oar, to each other, and to their bench, sleeping for short periods over their oar. The galleys, depending on speed, carried the absolute minimum of provisions, and the slaves survived on hard, coarse bread and a little water. Often slaves could not organize even movement to the rail to defecate. The stench was horrendous. The galleys carried rats, bedbugs, and fleas. This regimen went on for weeks as galleys pursued ships or attacked coasts. Rowers who died were unceremoniously thrown overboard. Slave galleys might undertake a second expedition in a season if pickings had been particularly good or if the slaver was unable to capture a prize the first time out. Contemporary observers, including slaves, thought that the Ottoman and French fleets represented the absolute worst of galley slavery; neither power permitted rowers off their ships for years at a time.

Once back in a port, such as Algiers or Salé, a galley slave's life improved in marginal ways. Though the stench and overcrowding of the public prisons appalled visitors, slaves usually had water to drink and could sleep through the night. They were not always chained, and there was a bit more food. The labor remained, however, hard, dirty, and dangerous. Salé, in Morocco, was always a smaller port. One seventeenth-century estimate put fifteen hundred as the peak figure for slaves there, far less than the twenty-five thousand at Algiers. Nevertheless, the work was largely the same. Slaves cut wood, mined minerals, made bricks, cultivated fields, and built sea walls and residences. Beatings were still frequent. Over and above the day's work, laboring slaves had to carry and sell water or hawk tobacco to pay for the meager fare that the slaveholder provided. At any time slaves accounted for approximately 25 percent of the population of Algiers and a somewhat lower percentage of Tunis, Salé, and Tripoli. One observer found the Salé prisons even worse than those in Algiers.

The social relations of Barbary slavery were more complex than merely those between a slave and his master. Any new slave entered an ongoing society. Failure to understand its rules and hierarchies could mean beatings or death. Slave prisons, like prisons everywhere, were organized hierarchically. Powerful and experienced slaves took the best jobs and protected their followers. It was essential to learn prison lingo quickly. Young men were claimed, raped, and then protected. Tensions inevitably surfaced in slave prisons. Protestant groups and Catholic groups hated each other. Catholic attempts to ransom slaves never included Protestant groups from northern Europe. One slave narrative, featured below, recounts the unfortunate experience of a North European Protestant slave who escaped from Algeria to Catholic Italy only to be sent to the Italian galleys as a heretic.

Surviving: Loyal Service and Conversion

Most slaves endured this bleak round of labor and galleys for years. A modern scholar has estimated that around 15 percent of all Barbary slaves died every year. Many of these fatalities were new slaves, not inured to the hard labor and bad food. The lot of some slaves slowly improved over the years of their captivity. A few were able to borrow capital from their masters and open taverns, frequented by Muslims legally forbidden both alcohol and tavern ownership. Slaves devised ways to make enough money to pay their master his monthly fee and have a bit left over. The most common tactic was to form gangs that stole from residents of the city. Some slaves carved wooden toys from scraps from leftover building materials and sold them through the streets. Slaves in private households, demonstrating loyal service, might move into less onerous work, such as taking care of children or buying staples in the market. These privileged house slaves dressed in the livery of their master, much finer clothes than the rough and tattered shirt and pants typical of laboring slaves.

It would seem that slaves who converted to Islam, known in Spanish as *renegados*, would immediately better their lot. Such was the case for skilled sailors and especially ships' officers. These elite *renegados* dressed like the elite of the city and moved about heavily armed. Their numbers were, in fact, small. They never formed more than a few percent of the population of Algiers in 1550–1640, the peak years of Barbary slavery. Such *renegados* usually found an investor willing to fit out a galley for slaving and raiding. Slave galleys were often successful precisely because their *renegado* officers were familiar with the waters and coastline they raided. In yet another irony of Barbary slavery, *renegado* captains sometimes raided their own home villages, in retribution for the village's failure to ransom them. Unlike skilled sailors, unskilled laborers who converted to Islam gained little. Masters resisted their slaves' conversion because a Muslim was legally forbidden to sell another Muslim as a slave. *Renegado* converts, therefore, could not be sold, and the owner was more or less stuck with them. The larger society accepted that a Muslim owner might have to beat or kill a Muslim slave, but such violence against a fellow Muslim was frowned upon.

Besides conversion, entrepreneurship, and gaining better jobs through loyal service, two other paths to a better life tantalized slaves. Escape was unlikely but not impossible. Groups of slaves occasionally stole a ship in a North African harbor, avoided re-capture, and sailed to a European port. During the period when Spain controlled a small enclave on the North African coast, some slaves walked long distances, eluded Muslim patrols, and reached freedom. It would be reasonable to expect that such slaves would be celebrated and feted in their home countries. On arrival in their home country, slaves first remained in quarantine for forty days. European countries feared bubonic plague, which was endemic in North Africa. After quarantine the slave's return was often celebrated with masses and processions. In Spain, France, and Italy, however, freed slaves sometimes faced the Inquisition. Close questioning, sometimes augmented by torture, sought to establish how "tainted" the slaves had been by contact with Islam and Protestantism, considered equally dangerous.

Escape and Ransom

Few slaves escaped Barbary, but tales of enslavement, suffering, and redemption developed into an enduring popular genre of literature across much of Europe. Barbary slavers and the slaves also appear, for example, in *Robinson Crusoe* and *The Count of Monte Cristo*, and a Mozart opera entitled (in translation) *The Abduction from the Seraglio*, which borrowed liberally from an earlier opera featuring escape from enslavement in a Muslim country. Slave narratives had common themes and structures, expected by their reading audience. They began with a straightforward account of the ship, its route, and items of trade. A detailed account of the encounter with the Barbary slavers followed. The ship generally ran, only to be overtaken and boarded. Much of the center of the narrative recounted the cruelties endured by the writer and his resistance to attempts to convert him to Islam. Many early capture narratives included

Members of the Order of the Most Holy Trinity and the Redemption of
Captives (popularly known as Trinitarians). During the height of the era
of Barbary piracy, it crisscrossed Europe, raising funds for the redemption of Catholic captive slaves. Today its primary mission is teaching.

unsubtle denigration of either Catholic or Protestant fellow captives.
Most slave narratives included a description of the round of daily work in
Barbary, but all focused on their "redemption" by which they gained their
freedom. Slaves were generally simply ransomed, but the most thrilling
narratives detailed the planning and executing of an escape and return to
Christianity. Few writers discussed their return to normal life in their
home country. Though these escape memoirs were popular reading at the
time, and several went through multiple editions, escape was, in fact, relatively rare. Robert Davis, a modern scholar of Barbary slavery, estimates
that only about 3 percent of Barbary slaves ever escaped.[10]

Ransom was somewhat more likely than escape, especially if the slave
was Catholic. A medieval Catholic order, founded in 1198 and known
as the Trinitarians, had dedicated itself to ransoming Christian captives. The order had been active throughout the later crusades in raising ransoms and trying to better the lot of Christian slaves. After about
1600, the Trinitarians focused attention on Catholic slaves in Barbary.
They established small chapels and hospitals in public prisons and raised

---

10. Davis, *Christian Slaves*, 21.

contributions in Italy, Spain, France, and ultimately as far away as Mexico for slave ransom. (Also active was another order, known as the Mercedarians, which sought ransom donations in Spain and Mexico.) Trinitarians, however, never raised the full amount of the demanded ransom. They contributed a fixed amount, which had to be considerably supplemented by money from a slave's family, through either petitions to their government or appeals to family members or friends. Much Trinitarian effort was spent in merely identifying slaves and making sure that the family money ransomed the right man. During the 1600s, the Trinitarians organized seventy-seven rescue missions, which ransomed perhaps sixty thousand slaves. This figure, however, constituted no more than 2 percent of the slaves of Barbary in that century.[11]

The Final Period of Barbary Slavery

Barbary slavery continued well into the 1700s but was on the decline from midcentury. Repeated bouts of plague had decimated the population of the North African ports. Rapid advances in technology and training, especially in England and France, produced sailing warships that were of formidable firepower, faster than the Barbary ships, and capable of serious shelling of a port. Both countries launched repeated campaigns against Barbary ships and especially Barbary ports and eventually extracted enforceable treaties that effectively ended Barbary attacks on their shipping, at least for a while. Attacks on Spain and Italy continue throughout the period. All the Barbary ports returned to slaving during the Napoleonic Wars (1803–1815), but this late adventure did not long survive the peace. The French entirely ended Barbary attacks on ships when they invaded and conquered Algeria and its Barbary states between 1830 and 1847. Before that happened, however, a new nation, the United States, found itself embroiled in two Barbary wars.

The United States and Barbary

The United States also had its sailors seized by Barbary slavers, who had captured ships and sailors based in the American colonies at least as early as 1625. Throughout the next 150 years, small numbers of American ships are recorded to have fought Barbary ships. Some escaped, but others were taken

---

11. Ibid., 19.

and their crews enslaved. In general, however, the treaties of Britain with the Barbary kingdoms protected the shipping of the American colonies, and there were decades when American colonial shipping was not harassed.

With the American Revolution of 1775–1783, British treaties with the Barbary kingdoms no longer covered the newly independent nation. Consequently, Barbary slavers seized the small schooner the *Maria* with its crew of six off the Portuguese coast in 1785. A narrative of one of those enslaved from this vessel is included in this chapter. Later in the same year the *Dauphin* was also captured. This new country founded on the idea of freedom and liberty watched twenty-one of its sailors enslaved. American newspapers covered the events and expressed outrage, but little was done. The American government had neither the resources to pay the ransom nor the navy to either patrol the Atlantic or attack the well-fortified ports of Tripoli and Tunis. The American sailors languished and died rowing galleys or dragging boulders for Tripoli's seawall.

Then, for almost a decade, a treaty involving Britain, Portugal, and the Barbary States protected American shipping. When this treaty expired in 1793, Barbary slavers once again seized American ships. Within a year of the expiration of the treaty, Barbary States had captured eleven ships and 105 American sailors, which provoked enormous publicity and a political crisis in the United States. More than a year of diplomatic negotiation between the United States and the Barbary States led to a peace treaty, which ransomed the American slaves held in Barbary for $1,156,000, one-sixth of the federal budget at the time.

Peace between the United States and Barbary lasted only until 1801 when the king of Tripoli demanded more money. The United States refused additional payment, and the Barbary States began once again seizing ships and enslaving crews. In 1803 the first U.S. military expedition against Algiers ended in disaster. The frigate *Philadelphia* foundered on shoals off Tripoli. The ship surrendered, and its entire 307-man crew was enslaved. Over the next fifteen months much of the American navy bombarded Tripoli, and a small force of Americans, allied with a substantial number of Muslim and Christian mercenaries, captured the key port of Derna. The two actions combined to force Tripoli's pasha (leader) to seek a peace treaty. Eight U.S. marines were at the center of the small invading force that captured Derna, and the Marine Corps still celebrates the victory in the second line of the *Marines' Hymn*, "to the shores of Tripoli."

The peace terms between the United States and Tripoli freed all American prisoners, but only after Thomas Jefferson's government paid a $60,000 ransom for the sailors. A second Barbary War between the

The American fleet attacking Tripoli in 1804. Clements Library, University of Michigan.

United States and Algiers lasted but four months in 1815 and resulted in another qualified victory for the United States. By the terms of the treaty, the dey (prince) of Algiers surrendered all American and European slave-prisoners, but the United States paid a "compensation" of $10,000, ostensibly for Algerian shipping that had been seized during the short war.

Clearly, these wars indicate that Barbary slavery was a form of state slavery, comparable to the state farms of the king of Ethiopia from the thirteenth century or haciendas in the Americas. Slaves were the most important form of capital for the state, and the state depended on slave labor and slave trading.

Let us now turn to narratives of British and American sailors who experienced Barbary slavery and to a satire by Benjamin Franklin that, by using the prism of Barbary slavery, lampooned arguments advanced by Southern slaveholders in the United States in defense of their "peculiar institution."

Sources

A Protestant Escapee in the Hands of the Inquisition

The author, Richard Haselton, was a sailor aboard the English ship *Mary Marten* in 1582, bound from London to a Turkish port in the

Mediterranean. On the return voyage two Barbary galleys attacked and sank the ship off the Cape de Gatte, the southeasterly most point of Spain. Haselton was taken aboard the galley, beaten, and taken to Algiers, where he was sold and rowed galleys for five years. He served aboard a Barbary galley, which was chased by Genoese ships near the Italian coast. The galley foundered in a storm, and of a crew of 250, only 15 reached land. The Muslims anticipated rescue by other ships of the Barbary fleet, but Haselton and two other Christians sought out local officials in hopes of freedom. We normally think of Muslim raiders enslaving Christian sailors and peasants. Haselton's story shows that the situation in the Mediterranean was quite complicated. Haselton, from England, was from a Protestant country. Spain, France, and Italy were Catholic and at war with England at the time. Rather than being saved by fellow Christians, Haselton was turned over to the Inquisition, whose representatives demanded that he recant Protestant beliefs and practices and accept Catholic communion and its implicit authority of Catholic priests. We pick up his story when he had been in prison for some weeks for refusing to recant Protestant beliefs.

Questions for Consideration

What might have been the audience for a memoir that showed Haselton's sturdy refusal to recant his Protestant beliefs? What other groups are mentioned as holding slaves on the North African coast? How far did the authority of the king of Algiers extend, if we can extrapolate from the memoir?

◆ ◆ ◆ ◆ ◆

Richard Haselton, *Memoir*[12]

I told him [the inquisitor] I would not do that which I knew to be contrary to the commandments of almighty God;

---

12. Richard Haselton, *The Strange and Wonderful Things That Happened to Rd. Haselton . . .* (London, 1595). Reprinted in Edward Arber, *An English Garner: Ingatherings from Our History and Literature* (London: Archibald Constable, [ca. 1910]), Internet Archives, accessed February 15, 2015, http://www.archive.org/stream/englishgarnering05arbe#page/n9/mode/2up.

neither had I been brought up in the Roman law, neither would
I submit myself to it. He asked me why I would not. I answered
that whereas in England, where I was born and brought up, the
Gospel was truly preached and maintained by a most gracious
princess;[13] therefore I would not now commit idolatry, which is
utterly condemned by the word of God. Then he charged me to
utter the truth, otherwise I should abide the smart.[14] Then was a
stool set, and he commanded me to sit down before him and offered me the cross, bidding me reverently to lay my hand upon it
and urged me instantly to do it, which moved me so much that I
did spit in the inquisitor's face, for which the scribe gave me a
good buffet on the face. So for that time we had no more reason-
ing. For the inquisitor did ring a little bell to call up the keeper
and carried me to ward again.

****

Then I asked him why he kept me so long in prison, which never
committed offense to them (knowing very well that I had been
captive in Argier[15] near five years' space), saying that when God,
by his merciful providence, had through many great dangers set
me in a Christian country and delivered me from the cruelty of
the Turks, when I thought to find such favor as one Christian
oweth to another, I found them now more cruel than the Turks,
not knowing any cause why. "The cause," said he, "is because
the king[16] hath wars with the queen of England" (for at that
instant there was their army prepared ready to go for England).[17]
Whereupon they would, divers times, give me reproachful
words, saying that I should hear shortly of their arrival in England, with innumerable vain brags which I omit for brevity.

And after, for the space of three weeks, I was brought forth to
answer several times every week. At which times they did sometimes threaten me with death, some while with punishment, and
many times they attempted to seduce me with fair words and

---

13. Queen Elizabeth I.
14. Undergo torture.
15. Algiers.
16. Philip II of Spain.
17. The Spanish Armada of 1588.

promises of great preferment, but when they saw nothing would draw me from the truth, they called me "shameless Lutheran,"[18] saying many times, "See, he is of the very blood of Luther; he hath his very countenance," with many other frivolous speeches.

After all this, he commanded to put me in the dungeon within the castle, five fathoms underground, giving me once a day a little bread and water, which they let down in a basket with a rope. There remained I one whole year, lying on the bare ground, seeing neither sun nor moon; no, not hearing man, woman, or child speak, but only the keeper which brought my small victuals.

[*Haselton eventually escaped the city through a watergate in the city wall, eluded capture for almost two weeks, but was captured and returned to the same dungeon.*]

The rack now standing ready. . . . Now I, willingly yielding myself, lay down. Then the tormentor bound my hands over my breast crosswise, and my legs clasped up together were fast tied the one foot to the other knee. Then he fastened to either arm a cord, about the brawn of the arm, and likewise to either thigh another, which were all made fast again under the rack to the bars, and with another cord he bound down my head and put a hollow cane into my mouth. Then he put four cudgels into the ropes which were fastened to my arms and thighs. . . . Then the tormentor, as he was commanded, began to wrest the ropes, which he did by little and little, to augment my pains and to have them endure the longer. But in the end, he drew them with such violence as though he would have plucked my four quarters in sunder and there stayed a good space. Yet to declare their tyrannical malice, thinking my torment not sufficient, he added more, pouring water through a cane which was in my mouth, by little and little, which I was constrained either to let down or to have my breath stopped until they had turned in such quantity as was not tolerable to endure, which pained me extremely. Yet

---

18. Haselton, an Anglican, was not a Lutheran. A follower of Luther was the catchall category that the Inquisition used for those who today would be called Protestants.

not satisfied, they took and wet a linen cloth and laid it over my mouth till I was almost strangled.[19]

[*Haselton survived the torture of the Inquisition and a public whipping. He managed to escape again, this time stealing a boat and sailing it to the coast of North Africa. A Berber tribe captured him, and its king offered him rich rewards if he would convert to Islam. He refused and went to prison. The king, however, noticed his carpentry skills in building gun carriages and framing houses and gave him considerable freedom of the city. Haselton's first attempt at escape from the Berber tribe failed, but the second succeeded, and he crossed river, desert, and forest to Algiers. Haselton was ransomed from Algiers in 1592 but gives no details of how this occurred.*]

◆◆◆◆◆

An English Slave in Algiers

William Okeley was an ardent Calvinist, whose capture and enslavement was a byproduct of religious and political strife in England. Charles I had dissolved Parliament in 1629 and generally oppressed the Puritans and other dissenting sects. Many of these Dissenters founded colonies in the New World in search of a better life, such as the earlier Puritan colony at Plymouth in 1620. In 1639 Okeley was in the Atlantic on a ship bound for a new colony on two islands off the coast of Nicaragua when his vessel was captured by Barbary slavers, and he was taken to Algiers. A wealthy man bought him and first used him for errands and other domestic service. His next tasks were carrying fittings for a new raiding ship his master fitted out, and nine weeks managing the cannon of this small sloop. The raiding expedition was unsuccessful, and Okeley's master demanded that he find some way to pay for his food and lodging, which he did, as

---

19. This was the same water-boarding technique that the American government used in operations in Afghanistan and in the Second Iraq War and decided was not torture.

this excerpt informs us. Eventually he was sold to another master and planned an escape before he had to move to the farm of his new owner. Okeley recruited six other European slaves. Against all odds, the group secretly built a foldable canvas boat. Okeley and four of the original six recruits took to the sea in this craft on June 30, 1644, and sailed for seven days, with virtually no provisions or water, to the Spanish island of Majorca. There, the viceroy took good care of the half-dead crew of the little boat. Thanks to the kindness of both Spaniards and English whom Okeley and his companions encountered in Majorca and on the Spanish mainland, they reached England in September 1644.

Questions for Consideration

What does Okeley's story about his servitude under his first master suggest about the complexities of Barbary slavery? If Okeley's second master was so kind, why then would Okeley undertake a dangerous escape in a homemade boat? Who do you think was his audience? Do you trust his description of his life as a slave? Explain your answer.

✦✦✦✦✦

William Okeley, *Memoir*[20]

My patron,[21] having been at great charges in fitting and manning out this ship, and the reprisals so slenderly answering his great cost and greater hopes, told me I must allow him two dollars per month and live ashore where I would and get it where I could.[22] This was a hard chapter that he that could not maintain

---

20. William Okeley, *Ebeneezer; or, A Small Monument of Great Mercy . . .* (London: N. V. Ponder, 1676), was first printed in 1675, thirty-three years after Okeley's return to England. The narrative was reprinted a year later, with a third edition in 1684 and a fourth in 1764.
21. His slave master.
22. The ship had failed to capture any booty or slaves during the raiding season, and the master was, therefore, short of cash to keep his house slaves.

himself should be compelled to contribute to the maintenance
of another. It was difficult to raise increase out of no stock and to
pay interest out of no principal, but there was no contending. It
cost me much debate with myself, and I turned my thoughts into
all forms and shapes, but all projects that presented themselves
were encumbered with so many difficulties that they amounted
very near to impossibilities. The more I consulted, the further I
found myself from a conclusion, and I could see no way but one
(but that was worth a thousand, could I have made the best of
it), and that was to commit myself to God, who had brought me
into this strait, beseeching Him that He would bring me out
of it. . . .

In this forlorn posture I wandered, but neither knew nor
much cared whither, though the wise God both knew and cared,
and His providence directed me to another Englishman who
was sitting in a little shop. He asked me, "What news?" And
(as that which is uppermost always comes out first) I presently
began the story of my desperate condition: how the rigid law of
my patron had imposed two dollars per month upon me, and I
knew not where to levy the least mite of it. He heard, considered,
pitied my condition, and invited me to come and sit in the shop
with him, but seeing nothing but bare walls, I asked him, "To what
end? What trade should we drive there? There's not much difference between starving in the streets and in the shop!" "Country-
man," said he, "I drive here an unknown trade. Here I sell lead,
iron, shot, strong waters,[23] tobacco, and many other things!" This
motion was a great deal too good to be refused, and I think at that
time no tolerable condition would have stuck with me.

I acquainted my patron with my design, pleaded I wanted
stock to set up with. He lent me a small modicum, and with
another pittance that I had privately reserved of my own, I began
to trade. That very night I went and bought a parcel of tobacco.
The next morning we dressed it, cut it, and fitted it for sale, and
the world seemed to smile on us wonderfully. In this way of part-
nership we continued for some while, and what we got clear, we
divided every week according to the proportion of our respec-
tive stocks. In a while, finding the world to come in upon us, we

---

23. Alcohol.

ventured upon no less than a whole butt of wine. Some money we had, and some credit. This wine we drew out and got considerably by it. But it's very difficult to maintain moderation in an exalted state, for even our state was capable of better and worse, for my partner, being elevated with our good success ... neglected his business, went tippling and fuddling up and down, and the concerns of the shop and trade lay wholly upon my shoulders.

It were tedious to trouble the reader how I wore out three or four irksome years in this way of trading. All this while there was no dawning of deliverance from our bondage. As one year left us, another found us and delivered us over captives to the next. Our condition was bad and in danger every day of being worse, as the mutable humors of our patrons determined upon us, for our shop and trade was no freehold. The truth is, in time we were so habituated to bondage that we almost forgot liberty and grew stupid and senseless of our slavery.

****

My patron had been sinking in his estate a pretty while; the last ship he had put to sea broke his back. At last he was grown (insensibly) so low that it could no longer be daubed up with his repute, but he must be forced to sell all his slaves to pay his debts. It was not much to me whither I was chopped and changed. I might change my jailer and my jail, but still I was like to be a prisoner. I might be bought and sold, and sold again, but still my condition was slavery.

I found not only pity and compassion but love and friendship from my new patron. Had I been his son, I could not have met with more respect nor been treated with more tenderness. I could not wish a friend a better condition than I was then in, except my bonds. If anything could be mingled with bondage to make it sweet, if anything could reconcile slavery to nature, if anything could beget acquiescence in such a state, I did not, I could not, want it. And indeed the freedom that I found in servitude, the liberty I enjoyed in my bonds was so great, that it took off much of the edge of my desire to obtain and almost blunted it from any vigorous attempt after liberty that carried hazard in its face, till at last I was awakened upon this occasion.

My patron had a fair farm in the country, about twelve miles from the city, whither he took me along with him. He had me to their markets, showed me the manner of them, and at my return he loaded me home with all manner of good provisions, that I might make merry with my fellow Christians. And I had some reason to conclude from his great kindness to me that he intended to send me thither to manage the farm for him. I saw now evidently that if I once quitted my shop, I should lose with it all means, all helps, and therefore all hopes to rid myself out of this slavery.

✦✦✦✦✦

An American Slave in Algiers

In July 1793, the American sailor John Foss shipped aboard the brig *Polly* bound for Barcelona. Algerian slavers captured the ship off the coast of Spain. His ship was one of ten American ships the Barbary slavers captured immediately after the expiration of the Anglo-Portuguese treaty. Foss and the crew of the *Polly* were taken to Algiers, put in prison, and each had a heavy chain attached to his leg. The following excerpt includes the daily round of work of slaves in the city of Algiers.

Questions for Consideration

How does this account of Barbary slavery differ from the earlier European ones? How do you explain the difference or differences? What does this account tell us about relations between the Ottoman Regency of Algiers and the United States? What does it tell us about the regency's relations with other nations? How does Foss define his identity? How does that identity frame his description of his enslaved experience? How far do you trust his description of the daily life of a slave?

✦✦✦✦✦

John Foss, A Journal, of the Captivity and Sufferings of John Foss[24]

At day break in the morning, the Prison-keeper calls all the slaves out to go to work, and . . . they are met by the Guardians or task-masters (who have their orders from the Guardian Bachi, who is the master of all the slaves that belong to the Regency) and we are conducted to whatever place he has directed.[25]

The greatest part of their work, is blowing rocks in the Mountains. While some are drilling the holes, others are digging the earth off those rocks, which are under it, and others carrying away the dirt in baskets. When the rocks are blowed, they take such as will answer their purpose: (Rocks less than twenty Tons weight, will not serve.) Many are hauled by the slaves, two miles distance, which weigh forty tons. They roll them to the bottom of the mountain, where is a convenient place to put them on a sled, from thence they are hauled to a quay,[26] about two miles distant, and left. . . . If anyone chance to faint, and fall down with fatigue, they generally beat them until they are able to rise again.

When a slave is found to be so sick that he is incapable of doing any kind of work, they then permit him to go to a hospital, until they think he can work again. This Hospital was erected by the Spaniards for the benefit of Christian slaves, in the year ———,[27] and is still maintained by them, when a slave goes in, he is used very well by the doctors and priests. They generally allow three or four doctors, and eight or ten priests to attend this hospital. The Doctors order what is to be given to the patient, and the Priests prepare it. While a slave is sick, he is no manner of expense to the Regency, for he is maintained with victuals, drink, medicine and attendance by the Spaniards; every morning one of the task-masters goes into

---

24. John Foss, A Journal, of the Captivity and Sufferings of John Foss, 2nd ed. (Newburyport, MA: A. March, 1798), 24–25, 119–20, 122. Available electronically from Gale Group, call number DS102997387.

25. The Regency of Algiers was established as Ottoman territory in 1525 and ended with the French invasion of 1830. See note 31.

26. A wharf. These stones were used for harbor and breakwater construction.

27. The date is left blank in the text.

"CAPᵗ CROKER HORROR STRICKEN AT ALGIERS, on witnessing the Miseries of the Christian Slaves chain'd & in Irons driven home after labour by Infidels with large Whips."

"Captain Croker horror stricken at Algiers, on witnessing the Miseries of the Christian Slaves chaind & in Irons driven home after labour by Infidels with large Whips." Engraving accompanying a printed edition of the 1815 report to "a member of Parliament" of Captain Walter Croker, R.N., regarding his experiences in Algiers while in command of the HMS *Wizard*. (CC-BY-SA 3.0 license.)

the hospital to view the slaves, and if he finds any one whom he thinks able to perform any kind of work, he drives him out, not even asking the Doctors whether they think he is able or not. And often times they are driven out in this manner, to work, and are obliged to return within two or three hours to the hospital again, and often expire within a few hours after their return.

****

At night when they have done hauling, all hands are called together, and have their names called by the Clerk, and every one must pass the Guardian Bachi, as his name is called. After they have done calling, and find that none are missing they are driven by the task-masters, into the city, and then left to go to the Bagnio,[28] by themselves, and must appear there within half an hour after they must enter gates of the city. The roll is called every night in the prison, a few minutes before the gates are locked. If anyone neglects his call, he is immediately put into

---

28. The prison.

irons hands and feet, and then chained to a pillar, where he must remain until morning. Then the irons are taken from his feet, and he is driven before a task-master, to the Marine,[29] and the Vigilhadge, (who is the Minister of the Marine) orders what punishment he thinks proper, which is immediately inflicted, by the task-masters. He commonly orders 150, or 200 Bastinadoes. The manner of inflicting this punishment is as follows, the person is laid upon his face, with his hands in irons behind him and his legs lashed together with a rope. One task-master holds down his head and another his legs, while two others inflict the punishment upon his breech, with sticks, somewhat larger than an ox goad. After he has received one half in this manner, they lash his ancles [sic] to a pole, and two Turks lift the pole up, and hold it in such a manner, as brings the soles of his feet upward, and the remainder of his punishment, he receives upon the soles of his feet. Then he is released from his bands, and obliged to go directly to work, among the rest of his fellow slaves.

****

I mentioned before, that on Friday, all the slaves work in the mountains, but on other days only a part of them work there. They have commonly a part of the captives at work in the marine. When they work in the marine, they have different kinds of employ. Sometimes they are cleaning the corsairs, and fitting them for sea. At other times they are stripping them, and hauling them up, discharging the prizes, cleaning the harbor, bringing those large rocks before mentioned, from the quay, on board a large flat-bottomed vessel. . . . And every article that is transported from one part of the Marine to another, or from the Marine to the city or from the city to the Marine, or elsewhere must be carried by the slaves with poles on their shoulders.

****

Nothing of any great moment happened after our arrival, which was on the first of Nov. 1793, until the eleventh, when

---

29. The harbor area.

a courier arrived from Alicant,[30] (sent by Colonel Humphreys, the Ambassador from the United States, for Algiers,) to obtain the Dey's[31] permission for him to come to Algiers, and make a peace. The Dey answered, that "he would not receive him, either to make peace or redeem the American slaves—that he had been soliciting the American government to send an ambassador to make a peace with the Regency for three years before, and they had treated his propositions with neglect—that as he had a truce with the Dutch and Portuguese, and had captured ten sail of American vessels, and had a fair prospect of capturing many more, he would not make a peace with them—that he made the truce with Portugal for the purpose of having the straits open for his vessels to cruize in the Atlantic, for capturing American vessels—that he could not be at peace with all nations at once."

****

On the 23rd of Dec. we were informed by Mr. Skjolderbrand, the Swedish Consul, that we were allowed a valuable supply from the United States. And he had that day received orders, and money, to pay each Capt. belonging to the United States, five Spanish Dollars per month, and each mate, and the rest three dollars each. Our country also furnished us with a sufficient quantity of clothing, decent and comfortable. This was happy news for us, for from the time of our being captured, to this day, we had been dragging out a miserable existence, scarce worth possessing with no kind of subsistence except bread and vinegar, and water to drink. This generosity of the United States to us their enslaved countrymen was of inestimable value. It was more precious from being unexpected. No nation of christendom had ever done the like for their subjects in our situation. The Republican government of the United States have set an example of humanity to all the governments of the world. Our relief was [a] matter of admiration to merciless barbarians. They viewed the character of Americans from his

---

30. Alicante, a city in Spain.
31. A Turkish title meaning "maternal uncle," the dey ruled the Regency of Algiers in the name of the Ottoman sultan. The dey at this time was Pasha Baba Hassan (1791–1799).

time in the most exalted light. They exclaimed, that "Though we were slaves, we were gentlemen"; that "the American people must be the best in the world to be so humane and generous to their countrymen in slavery." The goodness of my country I shall never forget.

◆◆◆◆◆

Benjamin Franklin's Satire on the Slave Trade

In his later adult life, Benjamin Franklin was an incisive and rational opponent of slavery and served as president of the Pennsylvania Society for Promoting the Abolition of Slavery. In the wake of a congressional debate over the issue of the slave trade, he penned his last public letter, which was published on March 25, 1790, in the *Federal Gazette*, only twenty-three days before his death on April 17.

In response to a petition to end importation of slaves into the new nation submitted by the Society of Friends (the Quakers), the House of Representatives of the First Congress debated the issue in 1790, which resulted in the finding that the Constitution prohibited Congress from any regulation of slavery until 1808. Always a humorist, Franklin connected the arguments for slavery brought forward in that debate and elsewhere in the United States with supposed similar arguments made by the slavers of Barbary a century earlier.

Questions for Consideration

How can one reasonably infer that Franklin composed this document as a not-too-subtle assault on the arguments of apologists for slavery in the United States? What were the apologists' arguments? How did Franklin endeavor to destroy them? Do any of the arguments seem to you to be ones that Barbary leaders might have made? What leads you to those conclusions?

◆◆◆◆◆

Benjamin Franklin, *On the Slave Trade*[32]

Sir,   March 24d, 1790

Reading last night in your excellent Paper the speech of Mr. Jackson[33] in Congress against their meddling with the Affair of Slavery, or attempting to mend the Condition of the Slaves, it put me in mind of a similar One made about 100 Years since by Sidi Mehemet Ibrahim,[34] a member of the Divan of Algers,[35] which may be seen in Martin's Account of his Consulship, anno 1687.[36] It was against granting Petition of the Sect called *Eriku*, or Purists, who pray'd for the Abolition of Piracy and Slavery as being unjust. Mr. Jackson does not quote it; perhaps he has not seen it. If, therefore, some of its Reasonings are to be found in his eloquent Speech, it may only show that men's Interests and Intellects operate and are operated on with surprising similarity in all Countries Climates, when under similar Circumstances. The African's Speech, as translated, is as follows.

"*Allah Bismillah, Etc.*
God is great, and Mahomet is his Prophet

"Have these Erika considered the Consequences of granting their Petition? If we cease our Cruises against the Christians, how shall we be furnished with the Commodities their Countries produce, and which are so necessary for us? If forbear to make Slaves of their People, who in this hot climate are to cultivate our Lands? Who are to perform the common Labours of our City, and in our Families? Must we not then be our own Slaves? And is there not more Compassion and more Favour due to us as Mussulmen, than to these Christian Dogs? We

---

32. Reprinted in Benjamin Franklin, *Autobiography, Poor Richard, and Later Writings* (New York: Library of America, 1987). Also found at http://sniggle.net/historicus.php.
33. Congressman James Jackson of Georgia.
34. Sidi Mehemet Ibrahim is fictional, part of the satire.
35. A somewhat tortured reference to the dey of Algiers. See note 31.
36. Samuel Martin, British consul to Algiers, 1672–1680.

have now above 50,000 Slaves in and near Algiers. This Number, if not kept up by fresh Supplies, will soon diminish, and be gradually annihilated. If we then cease taking and plundering the Infidel ships, and making Slaves of Seamen and Passengers, our Lands will become of no Value for want of Cultivation; the Rents of Houses in the City will sink one half; and the Revenues of Government arising from its share of Prizes be totally destroy'd! And for what? To gratify the whims of a whimsical Sect, who would have us, not only forbear making more Slaves, but even manumit those we have.[37]

"But who is to indemnify the Masters for the Loss? Will the State do it? Is our Treasury sufficient? Will the Erika do it? Can they do it? Or would they, to do what they think Justice to the Slaves, do a greater Injustice to the Owners? And if we set our Slaves free, what is to be done with them? Few will return to their Countries, they know too well the greater Hardships they must there be subject to; they will not embrace our Holy Religion; they will not adopt our Manners; our People will not pollute themselves by intermarrying with them. Must we maintain them as Beggars in our streets, or suffer our Properties to be the prey of their Pillage? For Men long accustomed to Slavery will not work for a Livelihood when not compell'd. And what is there so pitiable in their present Condition? Were they not Slaves in their own Countries?

"Are not Spain, Portugal, France, and the Italian states govern'd by Despots, who hold all their Subjects in Slavery, without Exception? Even England treats its Sailors as Slaves; for they are, whenever the Government pleases, seiz'd, and confin'd in Ships of War, condemn'd not only to work, but to fight, for small Wages, or a mere Subsistence, not better than our Slaves are allow'd by us. Is their Condition then made worse by their falling into our hands? No; they have only exchanged one Slavery for another, and I may say a better; for here they are brought into a Land where the Sun of Islamism gives forth its Light, and shines in full Splendor, and they have the Opportunity of making themselves acquainted with the true Doctrine, and thereby saving their immortal Souls. Those who remain at home have

---

37. Manumission is the freeing of a slave.

not that Happiness. Sending the Slaves home then would be sending them out of Light into Darkness.

"I repeat the Question, What is to be done with them? I have heard it suggested, that they may be planted in the Wilderness, where there is plenty of Land for them to subsist on, and where they may nourish as a free State; but they are, I doubt, too little dispos'd to labour without Compulsion, as well as too ignorant to establish a good government, and the wild Arabs would soon molest and destroy or again enslave them. While serving us, we take care to provide them with everything, and they are treated with Humanity. The Labourers in their Own Country are, as I am well informed, worse fed, lodged, and cloathed. The Condition of most of them is therefore already mended, and requires no further Improvement. Here their Lives are in Safety. They are not liable to be Impress'd for Soldiers, and forc'd to cut one another's Christian Throats, as in the Wars of their own Countries. If some of the religious mad Bigots, who now teaze us with their silly Petitions, have in a Fit of blind Zeal freed their Slaves, it was not Generosity, it was not Humanity, that mov'd them to the Action; it was from the conscious Burthen of a Load of Sins, and Hope, from the supposed Merits of so good a Work, to be excus'd Damnation.

"How grossly are they mistaken in imagining Slavery to be disallow'd by the Alcoran![38] Are not the two Precepts, to quote no more, '*Masters, treat your slaves with kindness; Slaves, serve your Masters with Cheerfulness and Fidelity*,' clear Proofs to the contrary?[39] Nor can the Plundering of Infidels be in that sacred Book forbidden, since it is well known from it, that God has given the World, and all that it contains, to his faithful Mussulmen, who are to enjoy it of Right, as far as they conquer it. Let us then

---

38. The Qur'an.

39. The first half of this "quotation" attributed to the Qur'an has been interpreted as a paraphrase of Sura 4:26 (Women), which requires that a believer show goodness and kindness to his slaves, just as he or she must to parents, relatives, orphans, companions, the poor and needy, neighbors near and far, and wayfarers. It is not known, however, whether Franklin had access to a translated Qur'an. Rather than paraphrasing the Qur'an, the passage may well be a parody of St. Paul's instructions to slaves and slave masters: Ephesians 6:5–9; Colossians 4:1; 1 Timothy 6:1–3. These three biblical texts were often quoted by defenders of slavery in the United States.

hear no more of this detestable Proposition, the Manumission of Christian Slaves, the Adoption of which would, by depreciating our Lands and Houses, and thereby depriving so many good Citizens of their Properties, create universal Discontent, and provoke Insurrections, to the endangering of Government and producing general Confusion. I have therefore no doubt, but this wise Council will prefer the Comfort and Happiness of a whole Nation of true Believers to the Whim of a few *Eriku*, and dismiss their petition."

The Result was, as Martin tells us, that the Divan came to this Resolution, "The Doctrine, that Plundering and Enslaving the Christians is unjust, is at best *problematical*; but that it is the Interest of this State to continue the Practice, is clear therefore let the Petition be rejected."

And it was rejected accordingly.

And since like Motives are apt to produce in the Minds of Men like Opinions and Resolutions, may we not, Mr. Brown, venture to predict, from this Account, that the Petitions to the Parliament of England for abolishing the Slave-Trade, to say nothing of other Legislatures, and the Debates upon them, will have a similar Conclusion? I am, Sir, your constant Reader and humble Servant,

Historicus[40]
The Federal Gazette, March 25, 1790

---

40. Franklin's pen name.

Chapter 4

Slavery Today

Old and New Slavery

Significant differences exist between slavery in the world before abolition and slavery today. Then, it was considered legal, moral, and the natural order of things. Peoples around the world successfully asserted that slavery was part of their culture. They also claimed that slave ownership and the slave trade were essential elements of their economies. With the influence of the abolition movement and the very real power of European countries in their colonies, "old" slavery declined in the late nineteenth and early twentieth centuries. Full slave societies, such as Ethiopia and Barbary, and slave-using societies, such as the American South and the Ottoman Empire, shifted to other forms of labor, though conditions for many ex-slaves improved little. Today slavery is illegal in all countries of the world, and it is generally considered immoral and assumed to be a violation of the natural right to freedom of all humans. Nations can no longer plausibly claim that slavery is purely a matter of "internal policy." They also cannot claim that slavery is an essential and inviolate part of their culture. Today a series of international agreements and United Nations statements define any person's basic freedoms anywhere in the world. These documents are supplemented by specific legal statements of the rights of children and the rights of women. Mechanisms are in place to initiate international economic sanctions to punish states that countenance slavery within their borders. These shifts in societal attitudes, national laws, and international agreements should have meant the end of slavery, but they did not. Let us first consider some exceptions to this general picture, where old-style slavery lives on.

Old Slavery: Mauritania

The nation of Mauritania is located in northwest Africa and encompasses a broad swath of the Sahara and some more productive land. Arabs from the desert regularly and routinely captured black Africans who farmed south of the Sahara, as well as purchasing them in towns and cities of the sub-Saharan kingdoms of Ghana, Mali, and Songhai, and transported them to the slave markets in North Africa. While the trans-Saharan slave trade has ended, slavery in Mauritania has not. So-called white Arabs still hold the descendants of captured blacks as well as dark-skinned Arab-Berbers, known as Haratin, as slaves and use them as labor in agriculture and herding, as well as prostitution and begging. Slavery seems part of a larger agenda of ensuring that Arabs retain power and blacks remain subordinated. Mauritania has passed anti-slavery legislation three times since independence from France in 1960, but the government, a dictatorship, has made no active attempts to end slavery. Mauritania is very poor, and Arab slave owners make the argument that a slave system is necessary to the economy—an argument that Benjamin Franklin parodied in 1790, as we saw in the last chapter. The ethos of slavery seems pervasive, and anti-slavery activists have observed that wealthier blacks also own slaves. Local anti-slavery organizations have received much harassment from the government and police, and the government has banned the term "slavery" from its newspapers. The United Nations has sent delegations to Mauritania but has done little else to end or alter slavery there. One modern scholar has estimated that there are today more than six hundred thousand slaves in Mauritania, 20 percent of the population, a higher proportion than any other country in the world.[1]

Old Slavery: Debt Bondage

Debt slavery is an ancient problem. Limits on its practice are found, for example, in the Pentateuch and in classical Greek laws. Typically, law codes limit the period of this form of self-slavery and lay out the conditions under which the debtor must become free. Social and economic conditions can, however, negate these limits, particularly in colonial situations. Debt slavery is today still widely found in South America, Southeast Asia, and India. Let us take India as an example.

In much of India in the eighteenth century, families owned and cultivated their own land. In most areas of the subcontinent, there was plenty of land. The scarce resource was people to cultivate it. In this situation it

---

1. See Kevin Bales, *Disposable People: New Slavery in the Global Economy* (Berkeley: University of California Press, 1999, 2004, 2012), chap. 3.

was difficult to gather enough labor for large-scale plantations.[2] Even the major indigenous export crops, such as pepper and cotton, were grown on a multitude of small, individually owned plots. The economy had some landless laborers, usually displaced from their land by war, famine, oppression by a ruler, or family quarrels. Typically, these landless laborers contracted to work for a farmer for a year or two. In a recovering economy they would likely be recruited to open vacant land and within a few years have become owners of small plots. Two factors changed in the second half of the eighteenth century. First, population increase meant that the great plain of North India finally filled up with farms occupying virtually all the available land. Second, the British conquered India and brought with them the principle of contract labor, which was quite foreign to India. British colonial judges misunderstood and misinterpreted existing rural agricultural labor relationships, in which landless laborers merely informally agreed to work for a farmer in return for a share of the produce, sustenance, and clothes. These new British courts, which the richer farmers were able to exploit successfully, interpreted these informal agreements as binding contracts, with specified wages, loans, interest, and obligations. The illiterate laborers had little idea of what they were signing. Within a century the result was millions of landless laborers who owed more than they could ever possibly pay and were, in effect, slaves.

After India gained its freedom from Britain in 1947, the new independent government recognized this debt bondage as a serious social problem and several times tried to end it. None of this legislation has in fact eradicated bonded debt slavery. There are, as we shall see in the source readings, probably still millions of slaves in this largely invisible system. In the poorest areas of the country, agricultural wages for landless labor can barely sustain a family. Typically a father borrows money from his employer for a wedding or an illness. Being illiterate, he cannot read the written terms or the rate of interest of the loan. Because the family never makes enough to repay the debt, the worker and his family cannot leave the farm of the debt holder. Any attempt to do so is met by violence.

---

2. There were, of course, large plantations in some areas, such as royal lands in Kerala and temple-owned lands in the south. Some scholars have argued that the rigidity and longevity of the caste system can be seen as a way to control the labor of outcastes for these big plantations.

Old Slavery: Child Exploitation

In many Asian, African, and South American countries, children must work to help poor families survive. This practice shades into slavery when a family, so desperate that it cannot feed or take care of its children, gives a daughter as unpaid domestic labor to a wealthier family or relative. In a similar route to slavery, a slaver promises the poor and desperate family that its child will be adopted by a rich family in a first-world country and have a much better life. This scenario may, in fact, occasionally be true, but it is not what usually happens. Typically the children end up as domestic slaves. When the girls should be in school they are washing endless laundry, carrying water, grinding grain, and cleaning the house. They are unpaid and kept in their "place" with implied and actual violence. Child labor, of both boys and girls, also weaves many of the carpets sold across the world. Much of this labor is so underpaid that it constitutes slavery, as the children should be in school, but they are bound to the loom for the entire day.

Old Slavery: Selling of Brides

At best, an arranged marriage matches a man and a woman who might well get along with each other and even love one another. Each family researches the potential mate for education, earning potential, physical attractiveness, and language. Families normally try to find friends who know the potential mate and his or her family. Negotiations center on dowry and making sure that the horoscopes of the potential husband and wife match. This sanguine picture, however, can and often does go awry. In some cases a wealthy older man essentially buys a young woman. Her family benefits from the transaction, but she ends up as somewhere between a concubine and a domestic slave.

The 1956 United Nations anti-slavery convention explicitly condemned dowry systems, that is, the exchange of money for a wife, which it defined as a "woman, without the right to refuse, is promised or given in marriage on payment of a consideration in money or in kind to her parents, guardian, family or any other person or group."[3] If, as many would

---

3. Supplementary Convention on the Abolition of Slavery, the Slave Trade, and Institutions and Practices Similar to Slavery, 226 U.N.T.S. 3, entered into force April 30, 1957,

argue, dowry is indeed a form of slavery, it is one of the most prevalent forms of slavery in our modern world. Dowry negotiations are typical in India and across much of Asia, the Middle East, and Africa. In India dowry is completely open and public, with expectations published in newspapers. Various initiatives by government and voluntary organizations have failed to stop it. If anything, middle-class dowries have gone up in recent decades.

Not-So-New Slavery: Political Servitude in Totalitarian States

War capture and enslavement, as we have seen, is as old as historians have records. It is documented in China, the ancient Near East, Egypt, Greece, and the pre-Conquest Americas. It often had an embedded notion of the "barbarian," the enemy alien, who could be morally and legally enslaved. Recall that in the Pentateuch, God guaranteed that the Israelites would defeat and enslave competing tribes. In the early thirteenth century, Chinggis Khan enslaved entire conquered populations, especially taking skilled artisans and engineers to his tent-city capital at Karakorum.

Forced labor was prominent on all sides in World War I, during which Germany used 2.5 million unpaid prisoners of war as slave labor in agriculture and industry. The forced labor camps were dismantled at the end of World War I, but Nazi Germany revived the operation in 1933 as a means of crushing dissidents and opposition.

In Hitler's Germany, this notion of ethnically and religiously inferior groups, properly enslaved, reached some sort of nadir in human history. Well before World War II, the nationalistic radical Right had defined Jews, Slavs, and Gypsies as inferior races, to be at best exterminated and at least enslaved. The use of slave labor was both a short-term tactic and a long-term strategy. By 1941, the Reich nominally "employed" more than three million in enforced labor from lands overrun by the Wehrmacht. For those originally recruited, the pay was trivial and the laborers were often kept in prisons, had to wear identification badges, and were not permitted out at night. The war itself, by the end of 1941, provided huge numbers of captured soldiers: a million from Poland, 1.2 million from France, 3.5 million from Russia to Nazi Germany. In 1941 Germany

---

section 1, article 1. The full text of the convention is available at http://www1.umn.edu/humanrts/instree/f3scas.htm.

repudiated the Geneva Conventions against the use of captured soldiers or civilians as slave labor. For Jews and ethnicities designated as "expendable," the camps were intended to kill, not just provide labor. This policy of "work to death" spread to Russians in the munitions works. By 1944, foreign, conscripted slave labor reached seven million, deployed in camps, in factories, and on farms. The tactic of bringing captured troops to work in Germany was, however, inconsistently applied later in the war. Of the five million Russians captured in 1944, more than three million died in incarceration and only 875,000 were ever actually put to work. Throughout the Nazi slave system, prisoners resisted as best they could, producing shoddy goods as slowly as possible. Tens of thousands simply walked away from their factories and farms every month, though the German military hunted down many of these escapees.

The Nazis articulated explicit racial and ethnic plans for slavery as a long-term strategy. Thus, there was a plan as early as 1941 for the creation of twelve thousand camps for the permanent enslavement of Slavs. Similar plans envisioned more than twelve million slaves for postwar construction projects. Albert Speer envisioned that Nazi Germany and its occupied lands would emerge from the war as a permanent slave state.

Nazi Germany was hardly the only polity in the twentieth century to use large-scale slavery as a political strategy. On the same scale as Hitler's use of slavery was Stalin's use of slave camps in Russia from the 1930s to the mid-1950s. Millions of dissidents, teachers, peasants resisting collectivization, ethnic groups, and religious minorities disappeared into these prisons, and few survived. Nearly two million were swept up in 1938 alone. When Russia took over Estonia, Latvia, Finland, and Eastern Poland in 1939, over a million of these new Soviet "citizens" were sent to the camps. Prisoners captured in World War II likewise entered the system, many held for years after the end of the war. Slave labor first built the camps and then the railroads and roads in the harsh, cold north. The system pitted slaves against each other, offering more food and a chance of minor advancement to those who informed on others. Slave labor worked the factories and farms throughout World War II. One of many ironies of World War II was Stalin's forming large military units based on his political slaves and committing them to the most dangerous engagements and tasks. They fought against Nazi units who re-enslaved them when they were captured. The state prison system actually expanded after World War II. More than 3.5 million people were in forced labor in 1946. The system continued at full strength until 1956 and gradually declined in numbers into the 1980s.

Larger in scale than either the Nazis or Stalin was Mao Zedong's use of slavery in China. The state used slave camps and enslavement in the countryside over decades as punishment for anyone perceived as a threat to the Communist Party: businessmen, slightly wealthier peasants, those supporting plans that the dominant party faction did not, teachers, students, and owners of property. Modern scholars have estimated that more than twenty million prisoners passed through some form of slavery in the last half of the twentieth century in China.

New Slavery: Trans-Regional and Trans-National Labor Exploitation

In the last century, large-scale changes across the world made a new form of slavery possible.

1. The poor became poorer, with fewer opportunities. The human population expanded as never before; common land became private agricultural land. The poor have found it increasingly difficult to survive by supplementing what food they could grow with food gathered from shrinking, jointly held grazing and forestland. As the available land closed so did a family's chances of betterment through its colonizing new land. Illiteracy remained high in villages.

2. Entrepreneurial activity shifted to the cities. New roads connected previously remote areas to growing cities. Transportation costs between regions and between countries dropped dramatically. What once might have been a four-month caravan trip became a four-hour airplane trip. The disparities in wealth between cities and the poorest areas of any country grew, as did the gap between the richest countries and the poorest countries.

3. War, often between regions or ethnic groups, became endemic, creating refugees and refugee camps.

All three factors combined to produce new areas of supply for slaves. The price of slaves, as measured against the cost of food or other necessities, dropped precipitously. Wealthier, more populous cities became demand centers for slaves, and new technology transported slaves more quickly and easily.

Defining the New Slavery

In this era of rapid communication, intense rural poverty, overpopulation, and refugees, modern-day slavery can only be defined by the situation itself, not the many circumstances that bring a person into slavery. Slavery depends on what happens when the person arrives. Is there a job waiting, or was the prospect of a job only a ploy to enslave the immigrant? Were communications from fellow townsmen or relatives correct or only a lure into slavery? Were the newspaper ads reflective of actual possibilities or completely deceptive? The slaver seizes passports, confines the people under his control, and sells them to a buyer. That buyer often transports the people to places to which they had no intention of going for exploitative purposes: women to brothels and unpaid domestic service and men to hard, dangerous physical labor. *Slavery exists when an "owner" can put a person into a work situation that pays nothing or almost nothing with conditions enforced and controlled by unconstrained threatened and actual violence. For the enslaved there is no legal recourse and little prospects of life getting any better.*

Both within countries and trans-nationally, many people are perfectly willing to exploit the weak and the poor. In the Barbary chapter, as we have seen, slavery was business, and slaves were commodities. Modern slavery is the same. While utterly immoral and illegal, like any other business, high-risk, high-return opportunities for profit can make slavery attractive to unscrupulous criminal networks. Patterns of slavery shift quickly. Changes in the supply of potential slaves might lower prices, changes in the demand for their labor might raise selling prices, or changes in the cost and dangers of transport to markets might make the trade more profitable in one country rather than another. The smuggler must figure out which police and border officials to bribe and how much to pay them. Smuggling of slaves also overlaps with smuggling of drugs, cigarettes, alcohol, and guns.

Modern slavery overlaps with many other social problems. Slavers, for example, often exploit the illiteracy of poor rural families, who cannot verify offers of jobs. The problems of the rural poor and the survival tactics of poor families vary even between regions of the same country. Discussion of modern slavery has been muddied by association with illegal immigration.

Nations are understandably concerned about illegal immigration. They would like to control their borders and document everyone crossing them. They would like to control access to jobs and social benefits in the country. There are, of course, criminal groups that specialize in trafficking, that is, moving people illegally across borders. This social problem is, however, different from the problem of slavery. People move illegally across borders for many reasons: seeking economic opportunity; fleeing war, religious oppression, or ethnic violence; or joining family members. These illegal immigrants do not necessarily become slaves. Even the supplemental definition of trafficking of persons "against their will" is murky. Perhaps a person began by agreeing to the trafficker's terms, but the terms change during the trip. The important point is that statistics generated by a nation on "trafficking" are not the same as the numbers of people in slavery.

This is a shadowy, criminal world. The only hard facts come from arrests and court cases. Worldwide, the number of convictions is relatively small. Both governments and organizations advocating for modern slaves periodically attempt to estimate the size of the current-day slave trade, but whatever is published is based on extrapolations, personal interviews, investigative journalism assessments, and a host of embedded assumptions. Beyond slaves actually interviewed and their stories, much of the literature must be treated as speculative. In discussing this rapidly shifting criminal world without reliable statistics, this chapter will consist of summaries of patterns and locations of slavery that are relatively well documented and studied, followed by documents that tell the stories of some modern slaves.

Chinese Slavery

In China a modern form of slavery begins with a criminal network, which signs contracts with people to smuggle them illegally to the United States or Europe. The illegal immigrant pledges years of labor to pay off the transportation costs. The relationship between a smuggler syndicate and a village is long running. If the syndicate is generally successful at smuggling villagers to the new country, more people from the village take out the contract. The arrangement is a grim proposition. The smuggler syndicate punishes the families of the person smuggled if he or she does not pay off the debt. It is often from desperation that the migrant leaves the village, and he or she may not fully realize that the new country is not a place of opportunity. Rather, the price of illegal immigration is years of slavery in the kitchens of Chinese restaurants. This bonded labor model does not automatically lead to slavery. If the bonded laborer pays off the debt, he is free, even if illegal, in the new country and can help his family back in China. If labor opportunities continue to develop within China along the lines of the past several decades, this form of slavery may rapidly disappear.

The Former Soviet Union

As in the Chinese case, slavery is the result of few economic opportunities at home. In the former Soviet Union, agents circulate in poor villages and towns recruiting both men and women with offers of well-paying jobs in Western European countries. Employment deception permeates the transaction from the beginning. The slaver paints a picture of a good job, such as in the travel industry, with film industries, as a club hostess, or as a nanny. Sometimes the recruiter is a well-dressed woman who claims to be returning to the area to "help" other women take advantage of the opportunities she has found. Men are recruited into what is ostensibly well-paid factory work.

Many young people are ready to leave their home areas because of limited job prospects and alcoholism in their own families. They assume that they can send money back to help the others. The recruitment story is a fraud, and the person is enslaved as soon as he or, more likely, she is in transit. Some of the women end up enslaved in brothels or as unpaid domestic servants in Holland or England. Some of the men end up not in factories but in barely paid agricultural work. If the slaver has seized passports, the slaves have few options. They generally do not know the local language and have no resources to return home. Even when advocacy organizations have located and helped these modern slaves, they have few good options. If the women return home, they are scorned as prostitutes and generally cannot find a husband. Unemployment remains as high as it was when they left. Many returned slaves leave again, hoping for more honest overseas recruiters.

Slavery in Brazil

Globalized, trans-national business can, even unknowingly, generate slavery. In the 1990s in Brazil, for example, the demand for steel in turn generated a demand for charcoal to manufacture the steel. Gangs of

workers made charcoal in brutal, dangerous conditions far into the rain-
forest. Not until word leaked out did anyone in the larger world realize
that the labor to make the charcoal had been recruited with promises
of high-paying jobs and that the charcoal workers were kept in locked
facilities and frequently threatened with violence. Their wages were con-
fiscated to cover inflated costs for housing and food. International publicity embarrassed the Brazilian government into action against slavers
in the charcoal industry. Conditions and contracts in the charcoal camps
are now monitored.

Sexual Slavery: Thailand and the World

In Thailand a poor rural family might designate one daughter to become
a prostitute in Bangkok. She would, thereby, fulfill her Buddhist obligation to support the family. Prostitution veers into slavery depending
on the conditions and the relationship between the woman and various
people taking a portion of her earnings: the bar owner, the pimp, or the
police. Sex work becomes slavery when a pimp or brothel owner takes
the money, beats the woman, and does not allow her to see her family or
find other employment. Though the sex district of Bangkok is still large,
profitable, and active, fewer of the women are Thai. Economic opportunities for factory and other work both in cities and smaller towns have
developed, creating alternatives to Bangkok prostitution for Thai women.
Many of Bangkok's prostitutes are now from poorer countries of the
region: Cambodia, Myanmar, and Laos.

One of the few points of consensus among researchers is that sex slavery
is a small part of slavery in the world as a whole and an even smaller part
of illegal smuggling of people across borders. One researcher estimates that
sex slavery is only 5 percent of worldwide trafficking. The U.S. Department
of State's *Annual Report on Trafficking of Persons* for 2010 suggests that
nine out of ten persons moved into conditions of slavery are in labor bondage, not sexual slavery. They are recruited to illegally cross borders in search
of better employment and subsequently have their passports taken, endure
physical threats and violence, and are forced to work for no pay.

New Slavery: Political Slavery from Below

In wars, especially civil wars, across today's world, many groups seize
and enslave children and turn them into fighters. This tactic has been

reported in more than twenty on-going armed conflicts. Estimates of the number of current child-soldiers vary widely, but a plausible guess might be a hundred thousand. Child soldiers have explicitly been used by resistance movements in Africa and South America, the Taliban in Afghanistan, and the Tamil Tigers in Sri Lanka. The typical child-soldier has been separated from his or her family, has little education, and identifies with the movement as his family and source of security. Once the war ends, it has proved especially difficult to reintegrate child-soldiers into society.

The Costs of Slavery

On the personal level the costs of slavery are enormous: physical damage, decreased health, depression and other mental problems, loss of childhood, and rejection by families even if the slave is freed. In sex slavery even if the woman escapes and is repatriated to her home country, often there is no work, just as there was no work when she originally signed on to work elsewhere. She is a shame and dishonor to the family, unmarriageable since many men have sexually used her. Re-trafficking is frequent.

At the societal level, slavery corrupts the place where the slaves came from: it undermines families—both nuclear and extended—and marriage patterns. It supports organized crime and subjugates young people who might demand change. Slavery also corrodes the location receiving the slaves. It undercuts free labor, funds organized crime and political corruption, and fosters the development of a culture of guns and violence. Slavery corrupts the police, who receive bribes and see the slavers as their "clients" rather than all citizens as their employers.

Slavery today, then, is a result of serious, complex, overlapping social problems that include poverty and landlessness, illiteracy, gender discrimination, ethnic and religious discrimination, dysfunctional families, and endemic warfare. Globalization often benefits only the rich and the middle classes and leaves the poor behind. Slavery is an outcome of these social problems, usually a cascade of several such problems simultaneously. As in earlier times, there are no "typical" slaves and there is no "typical" slavery. Patterns vary by region of supply, transport networks, and the eventual situation of the enslaved.

Changing Conditions

Fortunately, it does not take solving all these social problems to decrease slavery. The world changes quickly, and sometimes a region no longer has conditions that produce slaves. In Thailand, for example, the very work of the enslaved prostitutes, in an ironic turn, is decreasing the willingness of girls and families to send a daughter to the brothels. In the last decade, generally the first money sent back by a prostitute daughter in Bangkok to her rural family provided subsistence. Very soon, however, the family bought a TV. On TV was shown the dangers of AIDS and the urban life. Programs on TV challenged the image of the Buddhist dutiful daughter. Rural families are now far less willing to supply a daughter to the sex trade. At the same time, new types of jobs and industry have moved into northern Thailand, and education has become more available for women. The price of an enslaved young Thai girl has spiraled up. Brothel owners are looking to Laos and Cambodia for prostitutes.

Some success stories of positive actions to combat modern slavery also exist. In India, government policy and some crucial court cases have decreased debt bondage in most states. Publicity campaigns against several huge multinational companies, such as Nike and Coca-Cola, have largely ended their direct use of underpaid and slave labor. Even the charcoal industry in Brazil changed under intense scrutiny in the local press. Workers are no longer confined and are, by and large, paid for their work. Cocoa plantations in Africa, also because of adverse publicity, have largely ended slave labor. Would that these changes were universal, but they are not. Many of the systems and processes continue without noticeable change: child slaves crush rock by hand in Pakistan, weave carpets in Pakistan and India, and labor in prisons across the world.

Sources

The Legal Basis for Ending Slavery

At the end of World War II, the Allies discovered the scale of Hitler's genocide. It was felt that the protections afforded in the new charter of the United Nations to protect personal rights were inadequate. Eleanor

Roosevelt was one of the principal leaders calling for a statement of human rights, enforceable under the provisions of the United Nations. The countries on the commission that drafted the declaration were from around the world. The then forty-eight members of the United Nations adopted the declaration on December 10, 1948. The declaration did not, however, have the full force of law until 1976, when a sufficient number of member states had finally ratified it.

Questions for Consideration

In what ways do you find the *Declaration of Human Rights* different from any of the moral or legal documents of the previous chapters? According to this document, what rights belong to every person, by nature, not as a result of belonging to a particular religion, race, gender, language group, or ethnicity? Place this document in relation to other events at the end of World War II, such as the war crimes trials. How did they influence its principles?

A second legal document reproduced here is the specific convention on slavery and the slave trade that the United Nations adopted in 1956. How does this document connect debt bondage, unpaid child labor, and enforced marriage to slavery? How much more immediate and practical is this convention than the Declaration of Human Rights? Who is the audience for these documents? How do they relate to nationalism and the end of colonial rule?

◆◆◆◆◆

Universal Declaration of Human Rights[4]

Article 1.

All human beings are born free and equal in dignity and rights. They are endowed with reason and conscience and should act towards one another in a spirit of brotherhood.

---

4. United Nations, "The Universal Declaration of Human Rights," accessed September

Article 2.

Everyone is entitled to all the rights and freedoms set forth in this Declaration, without distinction of any kind, such as race, colour, sex, language, religion, political or other opinion, national or social origin, property, birth or other status. Furthermore, no distinction shall be made on the basis of the political, jurisdictional or international status of the country or territory to which a person belongs, whether it be independent, trust, non-self-governing or under any other limitation of sovereignty.

Article 3.

Everyone has the right to life, liberty and security of person.

Article 4.

No one shall be held in slavery or servitude; slavery and the slave trade shall be prohibited in all their forms.

Article 5.

No one shall be subjected to torture or to cruel, inhuman or degrading treatment or punishment.

Article 6.

Everyone has the right to recognition everywhere as a person before the law.

17, 2015, http://www.un.org/en/documents/udhr.

Supplementary Convention on the Abolition of Slavery, the Slave Trade, and Institutions and Practices Similar to Slavery, 1956[5]

Article 1

Each of the States Parties to this Convention shall take all practicable and necessary legislative and other measures to bring about progressively and as soon as possible the complete abolition or abandonment of the following institutions and practices, where they still exist and whether or not they are covered by the definition of slavery contained in article 1 of the Slavery Convention signed at Geneva on 25 September 1926:

(a) Debt bondage, that is to say, the status or condition arising from a pledge by a debtor of his personal services or of those of a person under his control as security for a debt, if the value of those services as reasonably assessed is not applied towards the liquidation of the debt or the length and nature of those services are not respectively limited and defined;

(b) Serfdom, that is to say, the condition or status of a tenant who is by law, custom or agreement bound to live and labour on land belonging to another person and to render some determinate service to such other person, whether for reward or not, and is not free to change his status;

(c) Any institution or practice whereby:

(i) A woman, without the right to refuse, is promised or given in marriage on payment of a consideration in money or in kind to her parents, guardian, family or any other person or group; or

---

5. Supplementary Convention on the Abolition of Slavery, the Slave Trade, and Institutions and Practices Similar to Slavery, Adopted by a Conference of Plenipotentiaries Convened by Economic and Social Council resolution 608 (XXI) of April 30, 1956, and done at Geneva on September 7, 1956. Entry into force: April 30, 1957, in accordance with article 13, section 1, http://www2.ohchr.org.

(ii) The husband of a woman, his family, or his clan, has the right to transfer her to another person for value received or otherwise; or

(iii) A woman on the death of her husband is liable to be inherited by another person;

(d) Any institution or practice whereby a child or young person under the age of 18 years, is delivered by either or both of his natural parents or by his guardian to another person, whether for reward or not, with a view to the exploitation of the child or young person or of his labour.

Section II. The slave trade

Article 3

1. The act of conveying or attempting to convey slaves from one country to another by whatever means of transport, or of being accessory thereto, shall be a criminal offence under the laws of the States Parties to this Convention and persons convicted thereof shall be liable to very severe penalties.

Article 4

Any slave who takes refuge on board any vessel of a State Party to this Convention shall ipso facto be free.

Section III. Slavery and institutions and practices similar to slavery

Article 5

In a country where the abolition or abandonment of slavery, or of the institutions or practices mentioned in article 1 of this Convention, is not yet complete, the act of mutilating, branding

or otherwise marking a slave or a person of servile status in order to indicate his status, or as a punishment, or for any other
reason, or of being accessory thereto, shall be a criminal offence
under the laws of the States Parties to this Convention and persons convicted thereof shall be liable to punishment.

Article 6

1. The act of enslaving another person or of inducing another
person to give himself or a person dependent upon him into
slavery, or of attempting these acts, or being accessory thereto,
or being a party to a conspiracy to accomplish any such acts,
shall be a criminal offence under the laws of the States Parties
to this Convention and persons convicted thereof shall be liable
to punishment.

✦✦✦✦✦

Debt Bondage

In the years after the passage of the *Universal Declaration of Human
Rights* and the Anti-Slavery Convention worldwide, the most common
form of slavery was debt bondage. This form of slavery did not have
many of the characteristics of older slavery. There was no violent war
capture, no moving of chained people over long distances, no slave markets, no enforced changing of names and religions. Instead, debt bondage slavery began with a simple local contract. The poor, landless man
agreed to work for a stipulated period for a local wealthy man—making
bricks or tilling the land—in return for an initial cash advance. What
turned the process into slavery were the terms of the contract, which,
of course, the illiterate poor man could not read. The interest rate and
the charges for housing, tools, and food made it impossible that the
poor man would ever be able to pay back the loan. He and his family
became slaves. The debt passed to his sons and daughters. Millions of
poor families were thus enslaved in India, Southeast Asia, Africa, and

South America. Much has been done to make debt bondage illegal in various countries, but until there are opportunities for better work, the conditions that produce debt bondage remain. Here is a summary of the statement from one bonded debtor in rural India who was technically free but has no real options.

Question for Consideration

Does this story provide any hint as to why Shri Dharma was still in dire economic circumstances even after he had paid off the principal and interest on his debt? Shri Dharma was fifty-five years old at the time of the interview (1989). In the early 1960s, he was a landless laborer in a village. Famine in his village forced him to the mines. Shri Dharma borrowed two hundred rupees from a man named Kishanlan but had no idea of the interest rate or the terms.[6] Decades later, unlike most bonded laborers, he managed to pay off the debt, but his circumstances improved but little.

◆ ◆ ◆ ◆ ◆

"I have three members in my family. I am the only earner. It takes 5–6 days to collect one truck [of] stones. After spending on gunpowder, etc., Rs. 15–20/- are left. I have my own hut. My wife is suffering from T.B. I am landless. If land could be given to me, I would prefer to return back [to his village]."[7]

◆ ◆ ◆ ◆ ◆

---

6. At the time the debt was incurred, the exchange rate was forty Indian rupees to the dollar. The debt was about five dollars, which, at the time, was about the cost of a Saturday-night date in the United States—pizza, a movie, popcorn, and gas.

7. Lakshmidhar Mishra, *Burden of Bondage: An Enquiry into the Affairs of the Bonded Quarry Mine Workers of Faridabad* (New Delhi, India: Manak Publications in association with V. V. Giri National Labour Institute, 1997).

Labor Exploitation in Europe

The following story, filed from Rome by Nick Squires, ran in the *Telegraph* (London) on April 26, 2010. Squires broke the sad story of a group of African men who had been recruited by the offer of well-paying industrial jobs, only to find themselves in agricultural work at less than minimum wage. Though the story was sensational for a brief moment, there was no follow-up to prosecute the network that recruited and brought the men to Italy.

Questions for Consideration

As you read this story, address the following questions: How does poverty and the lack of prospects relate these men to the bonded laborer in India? What problems of immigrant labor remain unsolved by simply turning the men over to an immigration center?

❖ ❖ ❖ ❖ ❖

"Mafia Ran 'Slave' Gangs in Southern Italy, Police Say"[8]

African farm workers were treated as little better than slaves by their mafia handlers sparking widespread riots, a police investigation into the violence four months ago has found.

Police said the clashes which broke out between black agricultural labourers and groups of white Italians in the town of Rosarno were fuelled by years of exploitation of the immigrants, rather than racial tensions.

Police arrested more than 30 people and seized farms and other property worth £9 million[9] at the culmination of an investigation into the violence in the southern region of Calabria in January, in which 53 people were injured.

---

8. Nick Squires, "Mafia Ran 'Slave' Gangs in Southern Italy, Police Say," *Telegraph*, April 26, 2010, accessed June 25, 2015, http://www.telegraph.co.uk.
9. Roughly $14,271,300.

Most of those arrested, on charges of mafia association and labour law violations, were Italians suspected of having links to organised crime.

The farm workers, who were mostly from sub-Saharan Africa, received no more than 25 euros (£22)[10] for working up to 14 hour days in the orchards and market gardens that surround the town, located on the toe of Italy's boot-shaped peninsula.

After arriving in Italy from Africa, often without the proper papers, the immigrants were exploited by local mafia gangs, who hired them out to farmers.

The labourers had to pay between six and 10 euros of their daily wages to their "agents." If they tried to go to the authorities, they were threatened with violence, police said.

"There was no sudden explosion of racism in Rosarno on January 7," said the local police commander, Carmelo Casabona. "The violence was instead a rebellion by foreigners against exploitation." An opposition MP, Rosa Villecco Calipari, condemned "an evil situation in which unscrupulous men force others to live in conditions of near slavery." Luigi De Magistris, an Italian MEP from the opposition Italy of Values party, accused the centre-Right government of turning a blind eye to an entrenched system of "modern slavery."

In the wake of the violence, hundreds of African men were evacuated from the area under police escort and taken to migrant centres, but many have since drifted back to their old jobs.

◆ ◆ ◆ ◆ ◆

Brothel Slavery in the United States

Human-trafficking victims in residential brothels are often forced to provide commercial sex to high volumes of men daily. In certain sex-trafficking networks, women and girls commonly "serve" as many as four men per hour, totaling forty-eight men in a given twelve-hour day. In this network, the victims are almost always women and children from Latin America. Brothels are typically located in homes, townhouses,

---

10. About $33 in 2015 exchange rate.

condos, apartments, and trailers. The majority of residential brothels are "closed networks" for only Latino men as "johns." Rather than advertising online or through newspapers, they distribute business cards, or *tarjetas*, and also publicize their existence through word of mouth.

The following is a paraphrase of a story by Jonathan Abel that was featured in the St. Petersburg, Florida, *Tampa Bay Times* in 2009. The arrests in the case provided access into a large-scale international network providing prostitutes for brothels in Florida.

Questions for Consideration

How does the role of misinformation relate this slavery to the plight of the African men in Italy? What other tactics do the slavers employ to maintain control over enslaved prostitutes? How does the story suggest the manner in which international networks deal with borders, laws, and police? How do the boundaries of nations both promote and inhibit this sort of trafficking? What evidence is required to prosecute slavers? When discovered, how are these enslaved sex workers best assisted?

✦✦✦✦✦

Sexual Slavery in Tampa, Florida

A Guatemalan woman was smuggled into the United States, first to a small town in Texas, then to Houston and Tampa, and finally Jacksonville. An enforcer told her that the fee had jumped from $5,000 to $30,000 and she had been sold to a brothel owner. In the brothel she turned twenty-five tricks a day, at $30 a trick, for the next eight months.

In police custody, the woman said that the brothel ring threatened her with both deportation and violence to her family in Guatemala, including her six-year-old daughter.

The brothel operation had likely begun at least five years earlier, smuggling Mexican prostitutes into Florida. A few years later the trafficking operation expanded to include women flee-ing poverty to work in the United States. Some of these women were forced into brothel slavery.

Local police and federal agents tracked the ringleader to Tampa and located his brothel there. Florida police cracked the operation and arrested not only the brothel owner but seven members of a prostitution ring that operated in several Florida cities, such as Tallahassee and Orlando.

In return for her cooperation in the case, the police con-tacted an organization specializing in assisting enslaved women, and they arranged medical help, contact with her family, and counseling on educational opportunities. At time of the article (2009), she remained in the United States and had moved out of Florida.[11]

11. Jonathan Abel, "How Clearwater Helped Destroy an International Sex Slave Ring," *Tampa Bay Times*, March 14, 2009, http://www.tampabay.com.

REFLECTIONS AND CONCLUSIONS

Slavery has been a degraded human condition found across history and across the world. Slavery has been typical of every type of economy: herding, shifting agricultural, sedentary agricultural, fishing, commercial, and industrial. Slavery has been found in every type of political system: tribal units, kingdoms, large empires, city-states, despotisms, fragmented states, communist states, and democracies. Slavery has been such a normal, culturally accepted, and legal feature of human societies that prior to the early modern era, none of the great religious thinkers, ethical philosophers, or jurists condemned slavery as morally wrong.

How might the condition of slavery be described? Slavery centers on ownership of one person by another. The ownership was often explicitly compared to ownership of an animal, a beast of burden, such as an ox or a camel. The master controlled a range of activities, such as what the slave ate and wore, what work he or she did and for how long each day, how the slave spent any free time, where the slave might go and when, the slave's education, and whether or not and often whom the slave might marry. Real violence, at the will of the master, followed breaking any of the rules.

A person could become a slave by many routes. In the long sweep of human history, the most common path into slavery was probably war capture. The victor swept up the defeated and reduced them to slavery. The Hebrew Bible and Roman law, to name just two examples, were clear and explicit on the right of the victor to enslave the defeated. Piracy and slave raiding were a variant of war capture. Professional slavers launched expeditions, on land and by sea, to capture men, women, and children as saleable loot, and slave markets brought slavers and buyers together.

Another route into slavery was the sale by desperately poor parents of their children. When famine stalked the land, slavery followed. A third route into slavery was by birth: once a slave, always a slave, generation after generation. Yet another route into slavery was self-enslavement, generally because of debt.

Even if the master wanted to keep slavery simple, the relationship between master and slave was destined to be psychologically tangled and complex. Slaves were humans, not beasts of burden, and the master-slave relationship was interlaced with the entire range of human emotions: not only lust, anger, greed, fear, and ethnic hatred but also guilt, compassion, affection, and pity. Slavery, however, affected much more than the master-slave relationship, influencing a society's legal, political, social, and economic institutions, its attitudes toward work, and even its moral and ethical foundations. If a society underwent a rapid increase in slaves, for whatever reason, slaves and the masters created a new society out of the situation.

Since slavery at some level has been found in virtually every human society, differences in how slavery was practiced were inevitable. The few "slave societies" had their entire economies based on slave labor. A high proportion of the population consisted of slaves, and the slave trade and sometimes even slave breeding were central to the economy. Wealth was measured mainly in slaves, and later historians cannot imagine the society's organization without slavery. Among our examples, the Barbary kingdoms of Algeria and Tunisia fit this pattern. Athens might have been a slave society, but the data are too scanty for us to be certain on this point. Strong arguments can be made that other slave societies included Rome in its classical period, Ethiopia in the period 1300–1800, the Sokoto Caliphate of West Africa in the nineteenth century, and the plantation states of the United States before the Civil War. The Ottoman Empire, where it is estimated that 20 percent of the population was enslaved, is an ambiguous case. We have argued elsewhere in this book that it was not a slave society, but the contrary can be reasonably argued. Most other societies only had some slaves and were not slave societies because slaves were a relatively low proportion of their populations; consequently, the society's economies were not based principally on slave labor. Moreover, the slave trade was not central to their economies, and wealth was not principally measured by the number of slaves one possessed. It is easy to imagine such a society carrying on more or less the same without slaves.

As an example of a society with slaves, let us consider colonial New England. With so much land available, it was always difficult to hire long-term contract labor on farms. The supply of free labor dwindled even more in the first decades of the eighteenth century as conditions in Europe improved and few were willing to sign indentured labor contracts, which traded passage to the colonies for seven years' unpaid labor. Farmers in many colonies turned to slave labor. In the middle of the eighteenth century, Massachusetts, Connecticut, and Rhode Island were the first colonies to enact legal slavery. The number of slaves in the northern colonies rose from about one thousand in 1700 to thirteen thousand in 1750. Farms in the northern colonies were, however, generally small with only a slave or two. Slaves also served in the cities in skilled trades, such as carpentry and baking, and in the households of wealthy masters. The Revolutionary War effectively ended slavery in the northern colonies. Some groups, such as the Quakers, actively opposed slavery, but practical concerns were equally important. Both the British and the Revolutionaries offered freedom to slaves who would serve in the army. Thousands did, and there was no going back to slavery after the war. After the revolution the white population of the northern states dramatically increased while the black ex-slave population decreased. Their labor was replaced by hired white labor, on farms, in trades, and in wealthy homes, without significant effects on the economic or social structure.

Just as the centrality of slave economics differed from society to society, so did the social organization of slavery. Even basic demographics differed from society to society. In the Barbary kingdoms, virtually all slaves were men, captured from ships and farms. In contrast, virtually all the slaves sold in markets in India in the eighteenth century were women, bound for domestic service in upper-class households. Even the life expectancy of slaves varied dramatically. The hard, dusty, dangerous work in mines, such as the silver mines of Athens, ensured that a slave's life was likely to be much shorter than that of a member of the free population. Many slaves on the Mediterranean galleys lasted only five to ten years. In other places slaves, such as those in domestic service in India or the Middle East, had a life expectancy that was probably about the same as the general population.

In all places and times slaves must have hoped for freedom, even when the only chance was escape through flight. Slave rebellions were a recurrent feature of world history, whether it was the uprisings of the helots of Sparta or the Zanj Rebellion near Basra. Some slaves escaped to mountains or forests and, beyond the law, established their own societies, such as the maroons in the Caribbean.

One of the most ancient extant law codes, the Code of Hammurabi, which we considered in the Introduction, recognized that slaves would flee and specified punishments for those who harbored runaway slaves. In many societies, however, a slave had a reasonable hope for freedom. Christian and Islamic traditions, for example, treat the freeing of slaves as a suitable act of religious merit for a man on his deathbed. Even Rome also had many freedmen among its population. In other societies, for example, ancient Athens, a skilled slave, say an ironworker or a shoemaker, had opportunities to make money beyond what he gave to his master. It seems that an Athenian slave might make enough to buy his own freedom. In the Ottoman Empire and other Muslim societies, the military slaves (mamluks, also known as janissaries in the Ottoman Empire) could reasonably expect eventual freedom and in the interim some of the privileges of freedom, such as advancement in job opportunities, even though they remained formally slaves. Even the predictability of the future for a slave varied considerably from society to society. In India in the eighteenth century, for example, women were sold into slavery only once and rarely resold. In the East African slave trade, in contrast, it seems that slaves were sold several times in the course of their lives.

The Barbary kingdoms, for example, forbade slaves to marry on religious grounds. The slave men were Christian, there were no Christian women to marry, and Christian men were forbidden to marry local Muslim women. The only way that a slave in this system might marry was to convert to Islam, which many slaves did. In many societies, however, slaves were encouraged to marry, even required to marry, since the master expected that the union would produce children and, thereby, more slaves. The slave plantations of the American South exemplify this feature of slavery, with the breeding potential of a male or female slave affecting his or her price. Jewish law assumed that every child of a gentile, or non-Jewish, slave would be a slave, generation after generation. This was not true for Jewish slaves held by Jewish masters. Such slaves and their children had to be released in the Year of Jubilee. In many parts of the world, however, it was not a foregone conclusion that children of slaves would automatically be slaves. In Islamic tradition children were often freed along with their parents. Societies also differed in their respect for a slave family unit. In India a woman was generally sold with her children. In the American South slave families were frequently broken up and the slave parents and children sold to different masters.

The physical conditions of slaves also varied considerably. Among the harshest situations was galley slavery on the Mediterranean, where men were shackled not only to each other but also to their rowing bench. If the ship sank they simply drowned. Beatings were frequent, whether the slaves were at their oars or in prisons on land. Many slaves, however, wore no shackles and moved freely through the house, where they served, or in the larger society. Roman literature is replete with examples of household slaves on errands in the city for their master. In harems, such as in the

Ottoman Empire, beatings were probably rare. They would have compromised the beauty of the fabled Circassian women slaves, for which large sums had been paid. Societies also differed in the degree of permanent marking of a slave through disfigurement, such as cutting the ears or distinctive tattoos. Recognizing that such a practice would effectively prevent a slave from ever joining society, the Code of Hammurabi banned such disfigurement except in special cases.

In many societies a slave had no legal standing. He or she could not give evidence, initiate a court proceeding, or seek legal redress. This situation, however, was not universal. In both Greece and Rome, slaves had limited legal standing and could provide information even if they could directly testify in court only under torture. In Greece and Rome slaves were at least partly responsible for their own actions and not seen as merely a body owned by their master. This situation of a slave in Greece contrasts with, for example, the thirteenth-century Ethiopian law code, which denies a slave any legal standing separate from his master. In this Ethiopian code the laws on redress for damage a slave might do are intermixed with damage an owned animal might do.

To add one more level of complexity to our picture of slavery, many societies had several different categories of slaves at the same time. In India, for example, in the seventeenth century there were three distinct categories of slaves. The first was imported African slave soldiers who were widely used in the armies of Muslim kingdoms of southern and western India. The second category of slaves was termed *devadasis*, consisting of girls donated by their parents to Hindu temples as dancers and prostitutes. A third category of slaves was poor girls sold by their parents into domestic service or as singers and dancers in upper-class households.

In spite of differences in slavery between societies and various categories of slavery within a society, some generalizations about slavery hold true. Rarely was slavery an essential, unchanging feature of a society. Slavery was subject to the same historical forces as other situations associated with work. If equally inexpensive local labor was available, slavery generally declined or disappeared. In India, for example, slave armies declined in the seventeenth and eighteenth centuries, displaced by local groups that took up soldiering as a new part-time occupation. They planted crops, went on campaign, and returned to harvest crops later in the season. This cycle was considerably cheaper for a ruler than maintaining professional slave soldiers year round. The demand for slaves also went up and down with the commodities they produced. In the Middle

East, for example, the numbers of slaves kept as pearl divers rose and fell with the desirability of pearls in European and American fashion. One of the last great surges in slavery in the Middle East was for opening date plantations, in response to an early twentieth-century demand in the United States for dates at Christmastime. The demand for slaves was also affected by changes in technology. In the Mediterranean, for example, the demand for galley slaves dropped as technological developments made sailing ships faster and better armed, capable of outrunning or outgunning a rowed privateer. The privateers had to build the new sailing ships and drop galleys to continue their profitable depravations.

In the long sweep of human history, only once was slavery condemned and attacked by a strong ethical and political movement. The abolitionists in England, France, and the United States in the eighteenth and nineteenth centuries denounced the moral and legal core of slavery. Often coming from the ranks of religious Dissenters, such as the Methodists, Quakers, and Baptists, they condemned slavery everywhere as a fundamental violation of the relations between man and God and man and man. They, along with French thinkers associated with the French Revolution, asserted that the right of a human to freedom superseded all cultural forms and all legal norms of any specific society.

Slavery did not, of course, simply go away. The period of the strong anti-slavery movement in Europe was also the period of European conquest of much of the planet.

The ending of slavery and the slave trade was part of the justification for European conquest, but slavery was at the center of making European colonies profitable for settlers and investors. The most glaring example is, of course, the plantations of the New World. Less known were the coerced labor on tea, coffee, sugar, and rubber plantations in Asia and the notoriously brutal slavery in the Belgian Congo.

The bloody American Civil War and the subsequent Thirteenth and Fourteenth Amendments to the Constitution settled the issue legally in the United States. Legal change at the constitutional level, however, did not mean the end of slave-like conditions at local levels. Without capital, education, or prospects, many African Americans in the South became sharecroppers in conditions as coercive as slavery. They remained subject to fiercely discriminatory Jim Crow laws that restricted everything from use of public facilities to decent schools. In the North, discrimination was less obvious but almost as oppressive. Unions kept African Americans from higher salaries, and real estate sale covenants kept them in urban ghettoes. The civil rights movement of the 1960s and following ended Jim Crow and many other overt forms of discrimination, but even though slavery legally ended in the United States 150 years ago and great strides have been made over the past half century to complete the full integration of African Americans into U.S. society, the reality of discrimination and coercion continues today. African American men, for example, are far more likely to go to prison for the same sort of crime for which a white person will go free, and with their loss of freedom often goes their loss for life of certain basic rights of citizenship, such as the right to vote.

Regardless of these glaring inequalities and vestiges of what was once legal and accepted bondage, slavery in the twentieth century moved from being natural, legal, and unquestioned to being widely seen as illegal, immoral, and unnatural. The glaring exception to a general decline of slavery in the twentieth century was the emergence of states enslaving their own citizens as public policy. One prominent example is Hitler enslaving Jews, other minorities, and prisoners of war in factories, mines, and forests before and especially during World War II. Stalin drastically expanded political prisons in Russia in the 1930s and sent to them millions of dissidents and ethnic minorities. It is estimated that between 1929 and 1953, the height of the Gulag system, some eighteen million persons were sent to slave labor camps, with about three million of them dying while enslaved. The survivors were released, however, when their sentences of imprisonment expired. This Gulag system was finally dismantled in the 1960s. The Great Leap Forward and the Cultural Revolution in China featured sending millions of city dwellers and intellectuals into rural slavery. Several million of these slaves died of hunger. North Korea maintains a large slave-prison population, though its scale and composition is largely unknown to the outside world.

The late twentieth century also has seen the rise of several new forms of slavery, all nominally illegal and clandestine. The relative decline in the cost of international travel has promoted trans-national prostitution. In a low-wage country with high unemployment, such as Thailand or Azerbaijan, scams offer rural women high-paying overseas jobs in tourism or entertainment. When the women arrive in the new country, slavers seize their papers and force them into prostitution. Phony marriage brokers also serve the sex trade and domestic bondage. Women in Nepal or rural China receive offers of marriage from desirable-sounding men, who apparently have good jobs and houses. The women arrive expecting to be brides and are, in fact, forced into prostitution. Men in areas of high unemployment are also subject to similar slaving operations. They are lured with promises of good-paying factory jobs, only to be enslaved into hard, dangerous work when they arrive. In some situations the fraud happens after the job begins. In India, for example, poor rural laborers sign contracts for a fixed period, receiving the money at the beginning of the contract. This system is known as bonded labor. For many laborers the system works as intended. They pay off their labor obligation and are free again. For others, possibly the majority of bonded labor, fraud in the charges for housing, food, and interest means that the laborer will never be able to pay off his original bond. He is a slave, as will be his children who will inherit the bond. Combining state slavery and these newer forms of slavery, it is quite possible that there are numerically more slaves in the world today than at any previous time in human history.

On the positive side there has been substantial progress in the international community on formal agreements that condemn slavery in all its current forms. The right to be free is accepted as a fundamental right of all humans. No document is more eloquent on this topic than the Universal Declaration of Human Rights adopted after World War II. Every country of the world has signed the Universal Declaration of Human Rights. It can and must be the standard all are held to if slavery is to be eradicated in the twenty-first century.

Beyond declarations and resolutions, what can be done to help end modern-day slavery? Initiatives are possible at the personal level, in businesses and industries, by national governments, and at the international level. At the personal level, we can all be more aware of what we buy and the conditions under which the items are made. For example, an organization known as Rugmark now offers third-party certification that handmade rugs from Asia are not made by slaves or children. The certification is common in Europe and spreading to the United States. Fair trade coffee also certifies that no workers in its cultivation and processing are slaves or ill paid. We all have the right and obligation to ask whether slavery or any form of exploitation is embedded in any product we buy. We also have the obligation to publicize any information on slavery that we find. The Internet makes this simple and inexpensive. We also can follow news stories of slavery and express our disapproval of businesses if they are involved through a supply chain that involves enslaved or otherwise exploited workers. We can also support programs and organizations that oppose slavery with publicity, education, and local job opportunities, especially in rural areas.

At the national level, we can encourage our government to aggressively prosecute slavers and to pressure weak or unwilling governments to prosecute slavers within their borders. We can support foreign aid that is premised on a country's efforts to decrease slavery within its borders. Government programs to decrease rural poverty will help and should be supported.

At the international level, we can stay aware of and support new legal initiatives that address rapid changes in modern slavery, such as the growth of the child pornography industry and the use of children in drug manufacture and transportation.

We can also go to http://www.freetheslaves.net to discover how each of us can play a role in supporting efforts to free the enslaved and to dismantle some of the systems that allow slavery to exist as a blight on our humanity. Free the Slaves is an international nongovernmental organization that operates in India, Nepal, Ghana, the Democratic Republic of the Congo, Haiti, and Brazil.

The scholar and human rights activist Christien van den Anker has suggested five principles that should underlay any action to suppress modern slavery. They form a means for all of us to think about the problem of slavery and act on proposed solutions. In brief, she calls for

1. Respect for the rights of the victims;

2. Justice for all as the basis for policies and laws;

3. Respect for the ability of slaves to define their situation;

4. Change in global business to more equality between producers and consumers; and

5. Development of viable alternative livelihoods, especially in poor rural areas.[1]

Implementation of these principles is a guide to us all.

---

1. Christien van den Anker (ed.), *The Political Economy of New Slavery* (New York: Palgrave Macmillan, 2004).

BIBLIOGRAPHY

Introduction

The controversial speculation about slaves as part of the Neolithic Revolution is argued in Karl Jacoby, "Slaves by Nature? Domestic Animals and Human Slaves," *Slavery and Abolition* 15 (1994): 89–97. An excellent set of articles, broadly considering slavery in ancient and modern contexts, is Enrico Dal Lago and Constantina Katsari (eds.), *Slave Systems: Ancient and Modern* (Cambridge: Cambridge University Press, 2008).

For the basics on slavery in China, see E. G. Pulleybank, "The Origin and Nature of Chattel Slavery in China," *Journal of the Economic and Social History of the Orient* 1, no. 2 (April 1958): 185–220; James L. Watson (ed.), *Asian and African Systems of Slavery* (Oxford, UK: Basil Blackwell, 1980); and Maria Jaschok and Suzanne Miers (eds.), *Women and Chinese Patriarchy: Submission, Servitude and Escape* (Hong Kong: Hong Kong University Press, 1994). For Japan, see Thomas Nelson, "Slavery in Medieval Japan," *Monumenta Nipponica* 59, no. 4 (2004): 463–92. For Korea, see William E. Henthorn, *A History of Korea* (New York: Free Press, 1971). For Southeast Asia, see Anthony Reid (ed.), *Slavery, Bondage and Dependency in Southeast Asia* (St. Lucia, Australia: University of Queensland Press, 1983). For India, see Richard M. Eaton and Indrani Chatterjee (eds.), *Slavery and South Asian History* (Bloomington: Indiana University Press, 2006). On the Inca, see Craig Morris and Donald E. Thompson, *Huáunco Pampa: An Inca City and Its Hinterland* (London: Thames and Hudson, 1985); and Sue Grosbill ("and he said in the time of the Ynga, they paid tribute and served the Ynga") in Michael A. Malpass, *Provincial Inca* (Iowa City: University of Iowa Press, 1993), 69–71.

Slave conditions in the Ottoman Empire, which included grueling agricultural work, rowing the galleys, and domestic drudgework, also included powerful slave concubines in the harem and slaves as commanders in elite slave armies. See Colin Imber, *The Ottoman Empire, 1300–1650* (New York: Palgrave Macmillan, 2002); and Ehud R. Toledano, "The Concept of Slavery in Ottoman and Other Muslim Societies: Dichotomy or Continuum," in Miura Toru and John Edwards Phillips (eds.), *Slave Elites in the Middle East and Africa: A Comparative Study* (London: Kegan Paul International, 2000). There is considerable recent scholarly literature on the slave elites in the Ottoman Empire and Mamluk

Egypt. See Shaun Marmon, *Eunuchs and Sacred Boundaries in the Middle East* (New York: Oxford University Press, 1995); Leslie Pierce, *The Imperial Harem: Women and Sovereignty in the Ottoman Empire* (New York: Cambridge University Press, 1993); and Ehud R. Toledano, *As If Silent and Absent: Bonds of Enslavement in the Islamic Middle East* (New Haven, CT: Yale University Press, 2007).

For slavery in medieval Europe and its decline, see William D. Phillips, Jr., *Slavery from Roman Times to the Early Transatlantic Trade* (Minneapolis: University of Minnesota Press, 1985). For the Church's position and European discussion of slavery, see David B. Davis, *The Problem of Slavery in Western Culture* (Ithaca, NY: Cornell University Press, 1966). An excellent introduction to the abolition movement is Seymour Drescher, *Abolition: A History of Slavery and Antislavery* (Cambridge: Cambridge University Press, 2009).

Most recently, the *Cambridge World History of Slavery* has produced two of its projected four volumes: volume 1, *The Ancient Mediterranean World* (Cambridge: Cambridge University Press, 2011), and volume 3, *AD 1420–AD 1804* (Cambridge: Cambridge University Press, 2011). Each volume is a collection of essays by acknowledged experts in the field on various aspects of global slavery.

Chapter One: Slavery in Ancient Athens

A good general introduction to ancient Greece is Sarah B. Pomeroy, Walter Donlan, Stanley M. Burstein, and Jennifer Tolbert Roberts, *Ancient Greece: A Political, Social, and Cultural History* (New York: Oxford University Press, 1999). For a survey of Greek slavery, see Yvon Garland, *Slavery in Ancient Greece*, rev. ed. (Ithaca, NY: Cornell University Press, 1988); and N. R. E. Fisher, *Slavery in Classical Greece* (London: Bristol Classical Press, 1993). The latter book, which is short, stimulating, and nuanced, is aimed at an undergraduate audience. Another useful discussion is Robin Osborne, "The Economics and Politics of Slavery in Athens," in Robin Osborne, *Athens and Athenian Democracy* (Cambridge: Cambridge University Press, 2010). Still important is Moses Finley, *The Ancient Economy*, updated ed. (Berkeley: University of California Press, 1999).

All writers on Athenian slavery have noticed the threadbare quality of the documentation. The debate over the number of slaves in ancient

Athens is far from over. Ellen M. Wood illustrates how taxation records show that a substantial percentage of Athenian citizens did not have the wealth to own even a single slave. See Ellen Meiksins Wood, *Peasant-Citizen and Slave: The Foundations of Athenian Democracy* (London: Verso, 1988). For the importance of slaves to the Athenian Economy, see Paul Cartledge, Edward E. Cohen, and Lin Foxhall (eds.), *Money, Labour, and Land: Approaches to the Economies of Ancient Greece* (London: Routledge, 2002).

For a broad comparison of Athenian slavery to other societies, see Orlando Patterson, "Slavery, Gender and Work in the Pre-modern World and Early Greece: A Cross-Cultural Analysis," in Enrico Dal Lago and Constantina Katari (eds.), *Slave Systems: Ancient and Modern* (Cambridge: Cambridge University Press, 2008). On the freeing of slaves, see Robin Osborne, "Religion, Imperial Politics and the Offering of Freedom to Slaves," in Robin Osborne, *Athens and Athenian Democracy* (Cambridge: Cambridge University Press, 2010).

Athenian law has justly received much scholarly attention. For a general introduction, see the chapter on slavery in A. R. W. Harrison, *The Law of Athens: The Family and Property* (Oxford, UK: Clarendon, 1968). See also P. A. Cartledge, P. C. Millett, and S. C. Todd (eds.), *Nomos: Essays in Athenian Law, Politics and Society* (Cambridge: Cambridge University Press, 1990). On slaves in the military, see Peter Hunt, *Slaves, Warfare, and Ideology in the Greek Historians* (Cambridge: Cambridge University Press, 1998); and Louis Rawlings, *The Ancient Greeks at War* (Manchester, UK: Manchester University Press, 2007). For the position of women, often compared to that of slaves, see Sarah B. Pomeroy, *Goddesses, Whores, Wives, and Slaves: Women in Classical Antiquity* (New York: Schocken, [1975]). On noncitizens, see Paul McKechnie, *Outsiders in the Greek Cities in the Fourth Century BC* (New York: Routledge, 1989).

Chapter Two: East African Slavery

Books that cover the general topic include R. W. Beachey, *The Slave Trade of Eastern Africa* (New York: Barnes & Noble, 1976); Murray Gordon, *Slavery in the Arab World* (New York: New Amsterdam, 1989); and Patrick Manning, *The African Diaspora: A History through Culture* (New York: Columbian University Press, 2009). Most recently, Matthew S.

Hopper, *Slaves of One Master: Globalization and Slavery in Arabia in the Age of Empire* (New Haven, CT: Yale University Press, 2015), looks at East African slavery in Arabia in the nineteenth and early twentieth centuries and examines the interconnection of slavery, empire, and globalization.

Useful documents on East African slavery are found in John Hunwick and Eve Troutt Powell, *The African Diaspora in the Mediterranean Lands of Islam* (Princeton, NJ: Marcus Weiner, 2002); and G. S. P. Freeman-Grenville, *The East African Coast: Select Documents from the First to the Earlier Nineteenth Century* (London: Rex Collings, 1962).

On the trade in Black Africans to Rome, see Frank M. Snowden, *Blacks in Antiquity: Ethiopians in the Greco-Roman Experience* (Cambridge, MA: Harvard University Press, 1970). The illustrations of Africans in Roman artwork are particularly valuable. Also useful is Phillip de Souza, *Piracy in the Graeco-Roman World* (Cambridge: Cambridge University Press, 1999).

On slavery in the Byzantine Empire, see Youval Rotman, *Byzantine Slavery and the Mediterranean World* (trans. Jane Marie Todd) (Cambridge, MA: Harvard University Press, 2009); and Demetrios J. Constantelos, *Poverty, Society and Philanthropy in the Late Medieval Greek World* (New Rochelle, NY: Astride D. Caratzas, 1992). The groundbreaking study of the role of eunuchs in Byzantine society is Kathryn M. Ringrose, *The Perfect Servant: Eunuchs and the Social Construction of Gender in Byzantium* (Chicago: University of Chicago Press, 2003). For further discussion of court eunuchs, see Judith Herrin, *Byzantium: The Surprising Life of a Medieval Empire* (London: Allen Lane, 2007), 160–69.

There has been much recent scholarship on the Indian Ocean and its trade. A selection includes K. N. Chaudhuri, *Trade and Civilization in the Indian Ocean: An Economic History from the Rise of Islam to 1750* (Cambridge: Cambridge University Press, 1985); Michael Pearson, *The Indian Ocean* (London: Routledge, 2003); Pius Malekandathil, *Maritime India: Trade, Religion and Polity in the Indian Ocean* (Delhi, India: Primus, 2010); and Kenneth McPherson, *The Indian Ocean: A History of the People and the Sea* (Delhi, India: Oxford University Press, 1993).

For slaves in early Muslim courts and armies, see Fred Donner, *The Early Islamic Conquests* (Princeton, NJ: Princeton University Press, 1981); Jacob Lassner, *The Topography of Baghdad in the Early Middle Ages: Text and Studies* (Detroit: Wayne State University Press, 1970); and Daniel Pipes, *Slave Soldiers and Islam: The Genesis of a Military System* (New Haven, CT: Yale University Press, 1981).

The primary material on the Zanj Rebellion is translated in Al-Tabari, *The History of Al-Tabari*, volume 36: *The Revolt of the Zanj* (trans. and annot. David Waines) (Albany, NY: State University of New York Press, 1992). An analysis of the rebellion is Alexandre Popovic, *The Revolution of African Slaves in Iraq in the 3rd/9th Century* (Princeton, NJ: Marcus Weiner, 1999).

The basic story of Malik Amber's path of enslavement is told in Radhey Shyam, *Life and Times of Malik Amber* (Delhi, India: Munshi Ram Manoharlal, 1968). More material on African slaves in India is found in Kenneth X. Robbins and John McLeod (eds.), *African Elites in India* (Ahmedabad, India: Mapin, 2006); and Indrani Chatterjee and Richard M. Eaton (eds.), *Slavery and South Asian History* (Bloomington: Indiana University Press, 2006). For mamluks, see anything by David Aylon, for example, his essay in Shaun E. Marmon, *Slavery in the Islamic Middle East* (Princeton, NJ: Markus Wiener, 1999) and his book *Islam and the Abode of War: Military Slaves and Islamic Adversaries* (Aldershot, UK: Variorum, 1994).

For slaves moving from Ethiopia to Yemen, see Emeri Johannes Van Donzell, *A Yemenite Embassy to Ethiopia, 1647–1649* (Stuttgart, Germany: Franz Steiner Verlag Wiesbaden GMBH, 1986).

Much has been written on the emergence of the Swahili trading culture on the East African coast. See John Middleton, *The World of the Swahili: An African Mercantile Civilization* (New Haven, CT: Yale University Press, 1992); and Mark Horton and John Middleton, *The Swahili: The Social Landscape of a Mercantile Society* (Oxford, UK: Blackwell, 2001). See also Abdul Sheriff, *Dhow Cultures and the Indian Ocean: Cosmopolitanism, Commerce, and Islam* (New York: Columbia University Press, 2010).

For the development of slavery and trading on the more southerly East African Coast, see I. N. Kimambo and A. J. Temu (eds.), *A History of Tanzania* (Nairobi, Kenya: East African Publishing House, 1969); John Gray, *History of Zanzibar from the Middle Ages to 1856* (London: Oxford University Press, 1962); Abdul Sheriff, *Slaves, Spices and Ivory in Zanzibar* (Oxford, UK: James Curry, 1987); Leda Farrant, *Tipu Tip and the East African Slave Trade* (London: Hamish Hamilton, 1975); William Geravase Clarence-Smith, *The Economics of the Indian Ocean Slave Trade in the Nineteenth Century* (London: Frank Cass, 1989); and Frederick Cooper, *Plantation Slavery on the East African Coast* (New Haven, CT: Yale University Press, 1977).

For the slave trade in the Ottoman Empire in the nineteenth century, see the following works by Ehud Toledano: *As If Silent and Absent: Bonds of Enslavement in the Islamic Middle East* (New Haven, CT: Yale University Press, 2007); *Slavery and Abolition in the Ottoman Middle East* (Seattle: University of Washington Press, 1998); and *The Ottoman Slave Trade and Its Suppression: 1840–1890* (Princeton, NJ: Princeton University Press, 1982). Each book includes some accounts by slaves, often given when seeking protection by the British in the Mediterranean. For the general story of British anti-slave trade naval patrols, see Bernard Edwards, *Royal Navy versus the Slave Trade* (Barnsley, UK: Pen and Sword, 2007).

For the aftermath of East African slavery, see Gwyn Campbell (ed.), *Abolition and Its Aftermath in Indian Ocean Africa and Asia* (London: Routledge, 2005); and Kwesi Kwaa Prah (ed.), *Reflections on Arab-led Slavery of Africans* (Cape Town, South Africa: Centre for Advanced Studies of African Society, 2005).

Chapter Three: Slavery along the Barbary Coast

The best overall survey of Barbary slavery is by Robert C. Davis, *Christian Slaves, Muslim Masters: White Slavery in the Mediterranean, the Barbary Coast, and Italy, 1500–1800* (New York: Palgrave Macmillan, 2003). Some new material, especially excerpts from slave narratives, is found in Robert C. Davis, *Holy War and Human Bondage: Tales of Christian-Muslim Slavery in the Early-Modern Mediterranean* (Santa Barbara, CA: ABC Clio, 2009). The most recent book on the subject is Adrian Tinniswood, *Pirates of Barbary: Corsairs, Conquests and Captivity in the Seventeenth-Century Mediterranean* (New York: Tiverhead, 2010), which underscores the fact that many of the Barbary pirates were European renegades. An older history is Stephen Clissod, *The Barbary Slaves* (London: Paul Elek, 1977). Mediterranean slavery makes a brief appearance in Fernand Braudel, *The Mediterranean and the Mediterranean World of Phillip II* (New York: Harper & Row, 1975). Useful for the middle period of Barbary slavery is C. R. Pennell (ed.), *Piracy and Diplomacy in Seventeenth-Century North Africa: The Journal of Thomas Baker, English Consul of Tripoli, 1677–1685* (London: Associated University Presses, 1989). For a view from France, see Gillian Weiss, *Captives and Corsairs: France and Slavery in the Early Modern Mediterranean* (Stanford, CA: Stanford

University Press, 2011). On slavery in Morocco in the nineteenth century, see Mohammed Ennaji, *Serving the Master: Slavery and Society in Nineteenth-Century Morocco* (trans. Seth Graebner) (New York: St. Martin's Press, 1998).

On the trans-Saharan route of slaves to North Africa, see John Wright, *The Trans-Saharan Slave Trade* (London: Routledge, 2007).

Slave narratives, which feature the details of daily life as a slave in the Barbary states, are found in two collections: Daniel J. Vitkus (ed.), *Piracy, Slavery, and Redemption: Barbary Captivity Narratives from Early Modern England* (New York: Columbia University Press, 2001); and Paul Baepler, *White Slaves, African Masters: An Anthology of American Barbary Captivity Narratives* (Chicago: University of Chicago Press, 1999).

The story of American involvement with Barbary is well told in Lawrence Peskin, *Captives and Countrymen: Barbary Slavery and the American Public, 1785–1816* (Baltimore: Johns Hopkins University Press, 2009). A longer-term consideration of American involvement with the Middle East is Michael B. Oren, *Power, Faith, and Fantasy: America in the Middle East, 1776 to the Present* (New York: Norton, 2007).

Chapter Four: Slavery Today

The first author to discuss modern slavery as different from older slavery was Kevin Bales, *Disposable People: New Slavery in the Global Economy* (Berkeley: University of California Press, 1999, 2004, 2012). He has continued to write persuasively on the topic. See Kevin Bales, *Ending Slavery: How We Free Today's Slaves* (Berkeley: University of California Press, 2007); and Kevin Bales, Zoe Trodd, and Alex Kent Williamson, *Modern Slavery: The Secret World of 27 Million People* (Oxford, UK: Oneworld, 2009). See also Alexis A. Arnowitz, *Human Trafficking, Human Misery: The Global Trade in Human Beings* (Westport, CT: Praeger, 2009); and Christien van den Anker (ed.), *The Political Economy of New Slavery* (New York: Palgrave Macmillan, 2004). A collection of photographs by Lisa Kristine, in *Slavery* (Washington, DC: Free the Slaves, 2010), offers graphic images of enslaved workers in Africa, India, and Nepal today.

A longer historical perspective is found in M. L. Bush, *Servitude in Modern Times* (Cambridge, UK: Polity, 2000). This author is the only one to consider state slavery as the largest slavery of the twentieth century.

On debt bondage, see Lakshmidhar Mishra, *Burden of Bondage: An Enquiry into the Affairs of the Bonded Quarry Mine Workers of Faridabad* (New Delhi, India: Manak Publications in association with V. V. Giri National Labour Institute, 1997).

On sex slavery, see Andrea Parrot and Nina Cummings, *Sexual Enslavement of Girls and Women Worldwide* (Westport, CT: Praeger, 2008).

On plans to end slavery, see Martin A. Klein, *Breaking the Chains: Slavery, Bondage, and Emancipation in Modern Africa and Asia* (Madison: University of Wisconsin Press, 1993); and Kwame Anthony Appiah and Martin Bunzl (eds.), *Buying Freedom: The Ethics and Economics of Slave Redemption* (Princeton, NJ: Princeton University Press, 2007).

Governments have produced voluminous reports on both slavery and trafficking, often with the two issues closely linked. See the U.S. Department of State's annual trafficking in persons report at http://www.state.gov/g/tip and "International Trafficking in Persons: Taking Action to Eliminate Modern Day Slavery," hearing before the Committee on Foreign Affairs, House of Representatives, 110th Cong., 1st sess., October 18, 2007, http://archives.republicans.foreignaffairs.house.gov/110/38332.pdf.

INDEX